SpringerBriefs in Law

SpringerBriefs present concise summaries of cutting-edge research and practical applications across a wide spectrum of fields. Featuring compact volumes of 50 to 125 pages, the series covers a range of content from professional to academic. Typical topics might include:

- A timely report of state-of-the art analytical techniques
- A bridge between new research results, as published in journal articles, and a contextual literature review
- A snapshot of a hot or emerging topic
- A presentation of core concepts that students must understand in order to make independent contributions

SpringerBriefs in Law showcase emerging theory, empirical research, and practical application in Law from a global author community. SpringerBriefs are characterized by fast, global electronic dissemination, standard publishing contracts, standardized manuscript preparation and formatting guidelines, and expedited production schedules.

Juan Pablo Hernández Páez

Mistake of Fact in Public International Law

Springer

Juan Pablo Hernández Páez
Faculty of Law
Universidad Francisco Marroquín
Guatemala City, Guatemala

ISSN 2192-855X ISSN 2192-8568 (electronic)
SpringerBriefs in Law
ISBN 978-3-031-59507-3 ISBN 978-3-031-59508-0 (eBook)
https://doi.org/10.1007/978-3-031-59508-0

This Springer imprint is published by the registered company Springer Nature Switzerland AG
The registered company address is: Gewerbestrasse 11, 6330 Cham, Switzerland

Paper in this product is recyclable.

To my dad,
Who taught me to own my mistakes;

And to my mom,
Who taught me to ask for forgiveness.

Acknowledgements

The idea for this book was born out of my experience in the Philip C. Jessup International Law Moot Court Competition in 2021. This detail will not be lost on any former participant who may be reading this. The case we faced was certainly special in its complexity. It concerned, in relevant part, a suspicious aerial incident, in which a small aircraft was shot down by the territorial State, who (incorrectly) believed it to be involved in a terrorist plot. As so many others, I was tasked with proving that this shootdown had been illegal.

But here's the catch: the aircraft, and the victims inside, all bore the nationality of the territorial State. So right at the outset, fundamental problems arose for us. Could you apply the Chicago Convention in such a case? Did I have standing to bring this claim? To what extent could my opponents rely on counter-terrorism law and jus ad bellum? An overwhelming feeling during the initial stages of the competition was that this incident appeared to be in a strange blind spot for international law. Of course, this feeling eventually went away. But it didn't make things easier.

In addressing these complicated aspects, my opponents would, eventually and without fail, raise the same key argument: the International Court of Justice should consider this to constitute one form or another of anticipatory self-defense, since the shootdown was intended to prevent a terrorist threat. I was always puzzled by this. See, even if a resort to force in these circumstances could fall within the realm of jus ad bellum, the aircraft was decidedly and objectively *not* involved in a terrorist plot. The victims inside were asylum-seekers, who failed to reply to urgent communications from intercepting aircraft due to a faulty radio. This had been all a mistake made by the territorial State, one that had been unforgivable considering the catastrophic aftermath.

My initial instinct was to challenge the idea that this had been an unfortunate mistake at all. I thought I could avoid this weird legal issue by claiming that the territorial State's mistake allegation was pretextual. It did not take long for my fellow teammates to scold me. Admittedly, this legal strategy forced me to stretch the facts of the case a little too far and had to be abandoned.

So, I was forced to face my legal demons. What if the territorial State did make a mistake? What happens when a State seemingly violates international law by mistake or accident? This made the argument of anticipatory self-defense even more puzzling for me. How can you claim to act in self-defense against a perceived, but objectively non-existent armed attack? Does this not expand the inherent right of self-defense too far? In my head, this was not, and could not be, *anticipatory* self-defense because, indeed, it was anticipatory to *nothing*. It could only be some form of imaginary or *putative* self-defense, a complicated notion that I had never encountered outside borderline cases of domestic criminal law.

Needless to say, this reasoning led me down a bizarre rabbit hole. It opened my eyes to a yawning lacuna in my understanding of perception and motive in international law. And, to my surprise, I came to realize that very few authors had addressed it outside the realm of international criminal law.

And so, here I am, almost three years later. Am I closer to the answer than I was back then? Perhaps slightly, but I will let you be the judge. This modest book should be understood as an attempt to put to the test some of the institutions of the law of State responsibility that I feel are too often taken for granted. It is intended to start a new conversation about the confines of international responsibility and our understanding of it. And I hope it compels the reader to ask herself, in international law as in life, are we not responsible for our own mistakes?

This book could not have been possible without my teammates from Universidad Francisco Marroquín (Jason Ruiz, Luis Pedro Arango and Marco Tulio León), who went through this legal ordeal with me and made the experience unforgettable. Special acknowledgement goes to Marco Tulio, my good friend and tireless opponent, who never hesitated to make my arguments impossible. Consider this my belated and long-winded rebuttal.

Guatemala City, Guatemala
2024

Juan Pablo Hernández Páez

Contents

Chapter 1
Introduction

1.1 Setting the Stage

By way of introduction to the topic of this book, imagine[1] that the fictional State of Andromeda has received credible intelligence that a terrorist attack will occur in the next few days. The attack will involve the use of a civilian aircraft that will be flown into government buildings in Andromeda's capital city. Sure enough, the next night, in the middle of a storm, a small aircraft breaches into Andromeda's airspace without clearance. Its general trajectory makes Andromeda believe that it is headed to the capital. All communication with the aircraft fails. Andromeda deploys two fighter jets with strict instructions to force the aircraft to land, with the purpose of detaining and questioning the pilots and preventing a potential catastrophe. When all measures short of the use of force prove inadequate, and the aircraft is mere minutes away from its apparent target, the fighter jets are ordered to shoot at the aircraft's wings to force it to land. The pilot loses control of the small craft and crashes in a forest near the city.

Later reports reveal that the aircraft was not involved in a terrorist plot at all. It had been forced to cross into Andromeda's airspace due to the stress of weather. The aircraft's radio had malfunctioned, and, in his desperation, the pilot apparently misinterpreted the fighter jets' visual instructions to land. Orion, the State of nationality of the aircraft and its passengers, protests the shootdown and indicates its intention to bring an international claim against Andromeda.

This hypothetical example poses a series of moral, political and legal conundrums. Was Andromeda entitled to use force against the aircraft? Is it liable for having misinterpreted the situation? Did Andromeda have any reasonable alternatives, like waiting

[1] Hypothetical example inspired by Question Presented IV of the 2021 Philip C. Jessup Moot Problem (*Case concerning the J-VID-18 Pandemic, Aprepluya* v. *Ranovstayo*), produced by the International Law Students Association (ILSA) and authored by Peter Tzeng. ILSA (2020), p. 17. This hypothetical fact pattern also resembles a series of accidental aircraft shootdowns that will be analyzed over the course of this book.

J. P. Hernández Páez, *Mistake of Fact in Public International Law*,
SpringerBriefs in Law, https://doi.org/10.1007/978-3-031-59508-0_1

for the aircraft to fly over the capital city, potentially compromising its national security? The government will be expected to investigate the incident and may be required to bring disciplinary or even penal action against the persons charged with making this fateful (and ultimately wrong) decision. But the question of blameworthiness does not only implicate the municipal law of that State. A case involving the use of lethal force against foreign aircraft and individuals will necessarily implicate also public international law, and its rules on the responsibility of States for internationally wrongful acts.

The primary rules at play will probably be rather clear. Assuming that both States are parties to these instruments, the State of Andromeda could be blamed for breaching the Chicago Convention on International Civil Aviation, the International Covenant on Civil and Political Rights and perhaps even the Charter of the United Nations. At the secondary rule level, however, the application of the rules on State responsibility may leave some readers with a distinct feeling of unease. Indeed, they may notice some unresolved issues. Yes, Andromeda did use weapons against a civil aircraft, but it did so under the credible belief that it was the victim of an attack by a terrorist organization, a threat that would have endangered the lives of its population and its territorial integrity. Andromeda could not have been expected to sit back and wait. But a survey of the available materials on State responsibility reveals that international law appears to be especially ill-equipped to handle this type of situation.

Unfortunately, this is a problem that cannot be sidelined. The number of cases involving mistakes committed by the State and leading to wrongful conduct is not small, and the consequences can range from lamentable to disastrous. Two distinct problems emerge from these 'mistake of fact' scenarios, from the perspective of the international law of State responsibility, which will be the object of this book.

First, there is a problem of definition. As will be explained later in this book,[2] modern international law tends to turn a blind eye to issues of fault (*culpa*) and malice (*dolus*) in the process of assigning responsibility to States, unless the primary rule under consideration demands it. The result is that the existing corpus of public international law on the issue of responsibility exhibits a lack of clarity, and a paucity of materials, when dealing with the role to be played by the State's perception and intentions. Consequently, there exists no unified notion of 'mistake' in the ambit of State responsibility.[3] This presents a methodological problem insofar as there is no uniform lens from which to analyze instances of mistake in the practice of States. Quite often, a 'mistake of fact' scenario is not acknowledged as such, which tends to complicate the analysis as to the legal effects that arise from the application of relevant rules.

Second, there is a problem of sources. Although recurrent factual paradigms can be identified, it is not yet clear whether this type of situation is addressed by any existing rule or rules of international law. The International Law Commission's work on

---

[2] See Chaps. 2 and 3.

[3] This is without prejudice to the issue of 'error' found in the law of treaties, see Article 48 of the Vienna Convention on the Law of Treaties (1969).

State responsibility does not seem to address this issue directly. Although invaluable academic contributions exist in the field of international responsibility and excuses,[4] there is a paucity of academic work dealing with the issue of mistakes of fact in the international law of State responsibility.[5] The extent to which other rules of international law, whose existence is less disputed, may bring an adequate solution to these factual patterns, is not clear either. The problem is compounded by the fact that, depending on the branch of international law under analysis, the relevant rules could exist at the primary or secondary levels.

The purpose of this book is to analyze the phenomenon of mistake of fact in public international law. In full conscience that this subject has elicited different responses in the various areas of international law, the focus of this book will be placed primarily on the law of State responsibility. The emphasis on secondary norms of international law is intended to aid in defining a unifying approach to this issue, which could be extended to the relevant areas of international law, except where *leges speciales* exist.

The structure of this book is as follows. This chapter will set out the analytical underpinnings of the mistake of fact phenomenon and lay the necessary groundwork. Chapter 2 will address the influence of a mistake of fact on the attribution of wrongful acts to a State. Chapter 3 will delve into how mistakes of fact may affect the existence of a breach of international law. Chapter 4 will evaluate the conditions under which customary international law recognizes the mistake of fact theory as a circumstance precluding the wrongfulness of a breach of international law. Finally, Chap. 5 will offer conclusions on the mistake of fact phenomenon in the international law of State responsibility.

1.2 Some Analytical Underpinnings

In the context of this book, a *mistake of fact* will be understood as an assumed fact or situation, which is later found to be incorrect. In other words, it is a false perception of reality, or a lack of awareness.[6] This means that the concept excludes situations of fraud or malicious misrepresentation from the scope of this book.

Additionally, this study excludes mistake of law from its purview. The distinction between the two concepts warrants some explanation. Perhaps the clearest way to separate mistakes of facts from mistakes of law is to review the application of Article 32 of the Rome Statute of the International Criminal Court, which regulates both concepts in the context of individual criminal responsibility for international crimes.[7]

---

[4] See *inter alia*: Paddeu (2018), Van der Wilt (2011), Kutoroff (2015), Kutoroff (2016), Haenen (2016), Crawford (2013), Kolb (2017).

[5] Sukumar (2021), Milanovic (2020a, b, c), Lahmann (2020), Trapp (2011). This is without prejudice to the more extensive literature about mistake of fact in respect of individual criminal responsibility.

[6] Triffterer and Ohlin (2022), para. 19.

[7] See Chap. 3 for further explanation of this provision.

Under this provision, mistakes are regulated as grounds to exclude such liability when they negate one of the constitutive elements of the crime—particularly, the mental element or *mens rea*. Van Sliedregt thus explains that in the Rome Statute system, the material elements of an international crime can be divided in two categories. *Descriptive* elements are those that can be perceived by means of the human senses, and *normative* elements are those that require interpretation or application of a legal rule.[8] Thus, while normative elements will relate to the construction and application of the legal rule applicable in the specific case, the descriptive elements are those that belong to material reality. In that paradigm, mistakes as to descriptive elements are always considered mistakes of fact.[9] Hence, lack of awareness or a misconception (or 'failed recognition'[10]) of a fact that constitutes a descriptive element of an international wrong will fall within the definition of a mistake of fact. This distinction has been pointed out by other scholars. For instance, Dubois and Vailhé have explained in the context of Article 32 of the Rome Statute that, unlike mistakes of law which implicate an erroneous assessment about a normative element of the crime, in cases of mistakes of fact the erroneous perception refers to a descriptive element. They give the example of a soldier that shoots in the direction of a hospital believing, due to bad visibility, that the envisioned objective was a military facility.[11] Similarly, Triffterer and Ohlin draw the same distinction and describe mistakes of law as a lack of awareness about legal elements.[12] They acknowledge, just like Van Sliedregt, that most elements have both descriptive and normative components.[13]

In the evaluation of mistakes of fact, a series of analytical considerations need to be made. Firstly, the cause of the mistake of fact will normally be decisive for the establishment of responsibility. That is to say, the practice indicates that an error caused by negligence on the part of the State or its actors will not be treated the same as one that is, for example, attributable to incomplete information where diligence was exercised to dispel the inaccuracy. This happens especially in cases involving emergencies, including those necessitating the resort to lethal force. In those situations, the State will need to adopt a decision on the basis of rapidly changing facts that lend themselves to errors discovered in hindsight. In the majority of cases, the mistake will not have a single, unifying cause, but will involve a series of interconnected factors that informed the decision of the State in the individual case. These situations are abundant in international life and the law needs to find mechanisms to account for them.

Secondly, the fact that the State is a juridical entity complicates our assessment. By definition, a mistake of fact exists in situations involving an error of perception on the part of the actor, which is difficult to ascertain when dealing with the institutional machinery of an abstract entity (a State) that acts through concrete beings (agents).

[8] Van Sliedregt (2012), pp. 269–270.

[9] Ibid., p. 271.

[10] Ibid., p. 271.

[11] Dubois and Vailhé (2012), p. 536.

[12] Triffterer and Ohlin (2022), para. 29.

[13] Ibid., para. 21.

This opens a variety of possibilities when it comes to how a mistake could be made, and which mistakes are relevant for the purposes of legal analysis. Is the agent's mistake, or the State's, that would trigger the application of an international rule? This may require appraising the conduct and perception of a large number of State agents, analyzing the role played by channels of communication within and outside governmental structures, and carefully surveying the institutional mechanisms put in place to avert such errors.

Thirdly, before analyzing any set of facts, it is important to solve the question of the applicable law. Different areas of international law will deal with mistakes in distinct ways. For some areas, a mistake that complies with a set of identified requirements may operate as a defense against international responsibility.[14] In others, the mistake itself will be the source of responsibility. This difference will turn on the law applicable in the specific case and the way in which that law handles mistakes of fact attributable to a State. One of the aims of this book is to analyze whether these different approaches can become compatible to create a unified theory of mistakes of fact.

References

Crawford J (2013) State responsibility. Cambridge University Press, The General Part

Dubois C, Vailhé J (2012) Chapitre 43. Les causes d'exonération de responsabilité. In: Ascensio H, Decaux E, Pellet A (eds) Droit international pénal. Editions A. Pedone (deuxième édition révisée), pp 529–541

Haenen I (2016) Justifying a dichotomy in defences. The added value of a distinction between justifications and excuses in international criminal law. Int Crim L Rev 16:3

Kolb R (2017) The international law of state responsibility: an introduction. Edward Elgar Publishing

Kutoroff A (2015) Emerging voices: excuse in international law. http://opiniojuris.org/2015/08/12/emerging-voices-excuse-in-international-law/. Accessed 16 Aug 2023

Kutoroff A (2016) Excuse in international law. Capital U L Rev 44:2

Lahmann H (2020) Mistake of fact in putative self-defense against cyber attacks. https://www.ejiltalk.org/mistake-of-fact-in-putative-self-defence-against-cyber-attacks/. Accessed 16 Aug 2023

Milanovic M (2020a) Mistakes of fact when using lethal force in international law: part I. https://www.ejiltalk.org/mistakes-of-fact-when-using-lethal-force-in-international-law-part-i/. Accessed 16 Aug 2023

Milanovic M (2020b) Mistakes of fact when using lethal force in international law: part II. https://www.ejiltalk.org/mistakes-of-fact-when-using-lethal-force-in-international-law-part-ii/. Accessed 16 Aug 2023

Milanovic M (2020c) Mistakes of fact when using lethal force in international law: part III. https://www.ejiltalk.org/mistakes-of-fact-when-using-lethal-force-in-international-law-part-iii/. Accessed 16 Aug 2023

Paddeu F (2018) Justification and excuse in international law. Cambridge University Press

[14] See, for example, Article 32 of the Rome Statute of the International Criminal Court.

Sukumar G (2021) Mistake of fact, interceptive self-defense and right to life. https://silpnujs.wordpress.com/2021/04/27/mistake-of-fact-interceptive-self-defense-and-right-to-life/. Accessed 21 Aug 2023

Trapp K (2011) Uses of force against civil aircraft. https://www.ejiltalk.org/uses-of-force-against-civil-aircraft/ Accessed 16 Aug 2023

Triffterer O, Ohlin C (2022) Article 32. Mistake of fact or mistake of law, 4th edn. In: Ambos (ed) Rome statute of the international criminal court: article-by-article commentary. Beck-Nomos-Hart, pp 1162–1182

Van der Wilt H (2011) Justifications and excuses in international criminal law: an assessment of the case-law of the ICTY. In: Swart B, Zahar A, Sluiter G (eds) The legacy of the international criminal tribunal for the former Yugoslavia. Oxford University Press, pp 275–295

Van Sliedregt E (2012) Chapter 10. Mistake of fact and law. In: Van Sliedregt E (ed) Individual criminal responsibility in international law. Oxford University Press, pp 269–286

Legal Instruments

Chicago Convention on International Civil Aviation. 7 December 1944. UNTS 295:15 [Chicago Convention]

Rome Statute of the International Criminal Court. 17 July 1998. UNTS 2187:3

Vienna Convention on the Law of Treaties. 23 May 1969. UNTS 1155:331

Other Documents

International Law Students Association (ILSA) (2020) Case concerning the J-VID-18 pandemic (United Republic of Aprepluya *v.* Democratic State of Ranovstayo). Order of 11 September 2020 (Problem, with Clarifications). https://www.ilsa.org/Jessup/Jessup2021/Documents/2021JessupProblem.pdf. Accessed 29 Apr 2022

Chapter 2
Mistake of Fact in the Establishment of Attribution

2.1 Introduction

In the process of analyzing the effects of the mistake of fact doctrine on the responsibility of a State, the first step is asking whether a reasonable and honest mistake may prevent such responsibility from arising in the first place. The framework within which one must examine this question is provided by Article 2 of the International Law Commission's (ILC) Articles on the Responsibility of States for Internationally Wrongful Acts, which provides as follows:

> Article 2
>
> *Elements of an internationally wrongful act of a State*
>
> There is an internationally wrongful act of a State when conduct consisting of an action or omission:
>
> (*a*) is attributable to the State under international law; and
>
> (*b*) constitutes a breach of an international obligation of the State.

This definition, which as recognized by the International Court of Justice's (ICJ) pronouncements in the *Tehran Hostages* case[1] is reflective of customary international law, requires two components for a 'wrongful act' to arise. First, the conduct under analysis needs to be imputable to a State in accordance with international law (*attribution*). Second, the attributable conduct must be contrary to an international obligation assumed by the State at the time of the conduct in question (*breach*). The ILC's Draft Articles on the Responsibility of International Organizations adopt a similar paradigm in Article 4.[2]

The concept of an internationally wrongful act proves to be a critical first step for any analysis of international responsibility because, as is recognized in Article

[1] ICJ (1980), para. 56.

[2] Article 4 of the Draft Articles on the Responsibility of International Organizations.

J. P. Hernández Páez, *Mistake of Fact in Public International Law*,
SpringerBriefs in Law, https://doi.org/10.1007/978-3-031-59508-0_2

1 of the Articles on State Responsibility and Article 3 of the Draft Articles on the Responsibility of International Organizations, 'every' such act by a State or international organization 'entails the international responsibility' of that entity. This may occur because the State's own organs have breached an international obligation; because the State is accountable for conduct of a non-State actor that is contrary to international law; or because the State has failed to perform a duty of prevention applicable to it (*responsibility by catalysis*).[3]

2.2 Mistake and Attribution

The question whether a mistake of fact can prevent the attribution of a conduct to a State is a complex one. It goes to the heart of the question of responsibility and its nature under international law. A mistake as to the facts of the case may be considered a factor that vitiates or even invalidates the intention or will of the actor. If one adopts the view that responsibility is subjective, a reasonable and honest mistake of fact may prevent such responsibility from arising, as the conduct under consideration was not born out of the actor's free will but an excusable error of appreciation. On the other hand, if one adopts an objective conception, responsibility arises by virtue of an objective link or attachment that exists regardless of the State's subjective intentions.[4]

This key difference manifests itself in a dichotomy that exists between the approaches adopted in most civil law and common law systems when it comes to national contract law. While the common law tends to adopt a theory of objective responsibility, where it is the mere breach of contract that matters,[5] most civil law systems adopt a subjective approach.[6] This approach relies on the existence of a 'ground' or 'factor of attribution' that gravitates around the party's blameworthiness or degree of misconduct.[7] The party in breach is responsible if the non-performance is due to that person's failure to observe the due diligence expected of her at the relevant time (negligence, fault or *culpa*).[8] Likewise, the person may be accountable to a greater degree if the breach was intentional or deliberate (malice or *dolus*). On the other hand, if the breach occurred against the person's will and not due to malice or negligence, that person may be excused; such may be the case of a breach of contract that occurs due to force majeure or *cas fortuit*.[9]

This conception of 'attribution' cannot be confidently translated into international law. Under the law of State responsibility, attribution is understood as the process of

---

[3] De Frouville (2010), pp. 277–280.

[4] Ibid., p. 268.

[5] See for instance Smith (2004), pp. 376–386.

[6] Schwenzer et al. (2012), para. 44.63.

[7] Ibid., paras. 44.72–44.73.

[8] Ibid., paras. 44.63–44.71.

[9] Ibid., para. 45.32; see Chap. 4.

attaching an act or omission to a State or international organization.[10] This step is essential because such entities are juridical in nature, and thus cannot act but through physical agents. Therefore, to determine whether an act breaches an international obligation, one needs to identify which actor is accountable for it, as otherwise the relevant international legal rule may not be applicable at all. This process of imputing conduct to the State or international organization relies on an objective fact of attachment: the status of the agent as a State or organization organ[11]; the control or direction exercised over the agent[12]; the government authority exercised by the agent, either by empowerment of the law[13] or in the absence or default of official authorities[14]; the conduct by insurrectional movements that become the new government or succeed in establishing a new State[15]; and the acknowledgement and adoption by the State or international organization.[16] In other words, the State's negligence, misconduct or malice does not enter into this calculation like it would in some systems of internal law. This is in line with the understanding that the modern law of State responsibility is based on a theory of objective responsibility.[17]

However, this does not mean that mistakes of fact are wholly irrelevant in the analysis of attribution. Some of the areas where mistake of fact may impact the imputation of an act to a State are described in the following sections.

2.2.1 *Theory of Appearance*

Under Article 4 of the Articles on State Responsibility, the conduct of any State organ is attributable to that State, if the agent is acting in official capacity.[18] The State is accountable even if the organ is acting against instructions or in excess of authority (*ultra vires*).[19] However, distinguishing between an individual organ acting in a private capacity and *ultra vires* acts may be challenging in practice.[20]

---

[10] ILC (2001), Art. 2, para. 12.

[11] Article 4 of the Articles on State Responsibility; Article 6 of the Draft Articles on the Responsibility of International Organizations.

[12] Article 8 of the Articles on State Responsibility.

[13] Article 5 of the Articles on State Responsibility.

[14] Article 9 of the Articles on State Responsibility.

[15] Article 10 of the Articles on State Responsibility.

[16] Article 11 of the Articles on State Responsibility; Article 9 of the Draft Articles on the Responsibility of International Organizations.

[17] See Chap. 3.

[18] ILC (2001), Art. 4, paras. 3–6.

[19] Article 7 of the Articles on State Responsibility.

[20] For some examples, see the awards handed down by the US/Mexico General Claims Commission distinguishing 'simple fraud' from 'excess of power', as cited and analyzed in De Frouville (2010), p. 264.

To fill this gap, international law employs the theory of appearance,[21] according to which the State must recognize that it is internationally accountable for conduct having the semblance of an official act.[22] This theory was described in the following terms by the ILC when considering what constitutes an "act of the State" according to international law:

> In international law, the criteria to determine whether the conduct of a State organ should be considered an act of the State itself, with all the consequences which follow therefrom, seem to be based essentially on the need for clarity and security in international relations which has so often been mentioned in the works of jurists, statements of position by States and the reasons given for arbitral decisions. (...) At the international level, the State must recognize that it acts whenever persons or groups of persons whom it has instructed to act in its name in a given area of activity appear to be acting effectively in its name within that sector. Even when in doing so those persons or groups of persons exceed the formal limits of their competence according to municipal law or contravene the provisions of that law or of administrative ordinances or internal instructions issued by their superiors they are nevertheless acting, even though improperly, within the scope of the discharge of their functions. The State cannot take refuge behind the notion that, according to the provisions of its legal system, those actions or omissions should not have occurred or should have taken a different form. They have occurred and, hence, from the international point of view they are actions or omissions of the State.[23]

It is when dealing with the possibility of limitation that one runs into difficulty. In his Fourth Report on State Responsibility, Special Rapporteur Ago reasoned that there may be some instances where, exceptionally, 'the acts committed by an official, although allegedly committed in the name of the State, are so completely and manifestly outside his competence, or fall within the scope of State functions so visibly different from those of the official in question, that no one could be mistaken on that score'.[24] This reasoning, based on a rule of 'manifest competence', would have allowed the State to avoid responsibility when the acts of the individual organ are so far outside of its sphere of authority, so *ultra vires*, that a reasonable third person could not mistake them for an act of the State as defined under international law.

Note that this reasoning should not be mistaken with the rule under the law of treaties that consent to be bound to a treaty can be challenged if expressed in 'manifest' violation of a fundamental provision of internal law.[25] The exception discussed by Special Rapporteur Ago concerned the attribution of responsibility for acts of State organs, and not the question of consent to treaty obligations, which the ILC itself has recognized as different matters.[26]

But the exception identified by Special Rapporteur Ago did not receive a sympathetic ear when the ILC was convened to consider his Fourth Report during its 27th session in July 1975. The ILC considered possible limitations of the rule providing

---

[21] De Frouville (2010), p. 263.

[22] ILC (1975), p. 67, De Frouville (2010), p. 264.

[23] Ago (1972), p. 93, para. 54.

[24] Ibid., para. 55.

[25] See Article 46 of the Vienna Convention on the Law of Treaties.

[26] ILC (2001), p. 39, para. 5.

for the attribution to States of *ultra vires* acts and reasoned that Ago's exception appeared to be based on the same logic as Article 46 of the Vienna Convention on the Law of Treaties. However, the ILC disagreed that this logic could be extended to the law of international responsibility:

> In justification of this conclusion it has been argued that if the lack of competence of the organ was manifest at the time when the organ acted, the injured party could and should have been aware of it and, in consequence, been able to prevent the illicit act from taking place. ... However, in the view of the Commission, the exception cannot be transferred just as it stands from attribution to the State of a declaration of will to attribution to the State of action liable to be the source of international responsibility. At the time of the conclusion of a treaty, if one party realizes that the organ of the other party is not competent to express the State's consent, it can always protect itself by refusing to agree to the conclusion of the treaty in such conditions. On the other hand, in the majority of cases at least, the fact of knowing that the organ engaging in unlawful conduct is either exceeding its competence, or contravening its instructions, will not enable the victim of such conduct to escape its harmful consequences.[27]

The ILC was then faced with a dilemma between two equally uncomfortable options. It could either introduce a full-blown manifest incompetence exception, which would 'run the unpardonable risk of presenting the State with an easy loophole in particularly serious cases where its international responsibility ought to be affirmed'[28]; or define a more limited exception excluding attribution when the victim should have been aware of the lack of competence and avoided the injury, which would reduce the applicability of the limitation 'to such a small number of cases that, in the end, it would only weaken unnecessarily the force of the basic rule which it is essential to confirm in the most positive fashion.'[29] Thus, the ILC decide to rule out the notion of manifest incompetence altogether:

> In conclusion, the Commission is of the opinion that, however worded, the limitation to exclude from qualification as acts of the State the actions of organs in situations of "manifest" lack of competence has no place in the rule defined in the present article.[30]

In this light, the attribution of *ultra vires* acts as it stands today appears to accept no exceptions based on the 'manifest' character of the lack of competence. The logical consequence of this is that, so long as the actor is a State organ, the State is accountable for its *ultra vires* actions, regardless of how obvious the lack or excess of authority. The law would then validate a mistake made by an observer that the State organ was acting within its sphere of competence and provide no way for the State to avoid the application of this rule by appealing to the unreasonable nature of the mistake. The inference of attribution drawn by the observer would be accepted by the law, regardless of whether it was mistaken from the perspective of internal law. In other words, international law would create some kind of irrebuttable presumption

[27] ILC (1975), p. 69, para. 25 (footnotes removed).

[28] Ibid.

[29] Ibid.

[30] Ibid (footnotes removed).

that the act makes the State accountable due to the status of the organ and regardless of the conformity of the organ's actions with municipal law forms and requirements.

What is not certain is whether the same rule of appearance applies to other grounds of attribution, e.g., to possible 'appearances of effective control'. When discussing the attributability of unauthorized acts in the realm of effective control, the ILC gives a cryptic answer. On the one hand, an unauthorized act under the effective control of a State that contravenes that State's instructions or directions is still attributable if it is 'incidental' to the performance of the instructions, but not otherwise.[31] But at the same time, 'where persons or groups have committed acts under the effective control of a State, the condition for attribution will still be met even if particular instructions may have been ignored.'[32] It seems that the rule expounded here is that one should not focus on whether the totality of the instruction or direction has been observed, but on the actual exercise of control, which seems reasonable. And the standard to prove the existence of that control would be high, as flows from the ICJ's findings in *Nicaragua*[33] and *Bosnian Genocide*.[34]

Yet, recent jurisprudence has not ruled out the possibility of attribution in exceptional cases where there is an appearance of effective control that is not dispelled by the controlling State. The example examined here is the *Carter* v. *Russia* case before the European Court of Human Rights. The case concerned the murder of Aleksandr Litvinenko, a former agent of the Soviet Union's Committee for State Security (KGB) and its successor agencies, including Russia's Federal Security Service (FSB), who defected in 2001 and was granted asylum by the United Kingdom. Following meetings with Andrey Lugovoy, owner of a Russian security company and former KGB officer, and his 'long-standing acquaintance', Dmitry Kovtun, Litvinenko showed signs of polonium-210 poisoning, which led to his death in November 2006. The poisoning was later found by the United Kingdom Government to have been committed by Lugovoy and Kovtun.

When analyzing whether Lugovoy and Kovtun had acted as agents of the Russian Federation, and therefore under its jurisdiction for the purposes of the European Convention on Human Rights, the Court looked at a series of factors. First, it had been established that Lugovoy and Kovtun were not acting on their own initiative, and indeed had no personal motive to kill Litvinenko; instead, they were ostensibly acting on the direction of another entity.[35] Second, Lugovoy and Kovtun employed polonium-210, a rare radioactive isotope that could not have been plausibly obtained by them without the support of a State entity, as it must have come from a reactor under State control.[36] Third, the motive for the killing suggested State involvement. Theories pointing at other actors or entities with an interest of killing Litvinenko had been discarded by the United Kingdom inquiry, which concluded that there

[31] ILC (2001), Art. 8, para. 8.

[32] Ibid.

[33] ICJ (1986a), paras. 115–116.

[34] ICJ (2007), paras. 396–412.

[35] ECtHR (2021), paras. 63, 69, 163.

[36] Ibid., paras. 64–66, 163.

was a strong probability that organizations and individuals within the Russian State, including its security service, had a motive to poison Litvinenko.[37] According to the Court, 'the identification of the perpetrators of the killing and the indication of their connection with the authorities of the respondent State established a strong prima facie case that, in killing Mr. Litvinenko, Mr. Lugovoy and Mr. Kovtun were acting under the direction or control of the Russian authorities.'[38] Fourth, while recognizing a 'theoretical possibility' that Litvinenko's murder might have been a 'rogue operation' not involving the Russian Federation, the Court determined that the information needed to refute its initial conclusion lay exclusively within the knowledge of the Russian government, who invoked constitutional protection against Lugovoy and Kovtun's extradition and failed to carry out a careful investigation to determine whether the two suspects had been acting under the control of a State entity. Thus, the Court drew an 'adverse inference' of effective control under Article 8 of the Articles on State Responsibility.[39]

The *Carter* case is an interesting example where an international tribunal relied on a 'semblance of effective control', as it were, to substantiate a ground of attribution. From the European Court's perspective, an objectively reasonable appearance of effective control, not refuted by the incumbent State, was sufficient to trigger attribution under Article 8 of the Articles on State Responsibility. The possibility that this ruling contradicted the ICJ's own understanding of effective control has been suggested.[40] Arguably, the conclusion would still be justified by appealing instead to Article 11 of the Articles on State Responsibility. But appraising the European Court's ruling on its merits, the semblance of effective control would still have led to the attribution of the conduct, even if it happened not to fully correspond with reality.

The possibility of validating a mistake of fact flows naturally from the existing rules on attribution in the circumstances described previously. For instance, in the context of its commentary to Article 7 of the Articles on State Responsibility, the ILC recognized the link between the attribution of *ultra vires* acts and the recognition of acts performed under the 'real' or 'apparent' authority of the State.[41] Moreover, the relationship that this theory bears with the rules on the taking and evaluation of evidence is also a factor to consider. Indeed, to reach a conclusion based on available evidence is a fundamental element of the judicial function of a tribunal. This does not mean that on occasion the tribunal may need to reach a conclusion through inferences without having the whole picture. Thus, the operation of these rules leaves ample space for potential misinterpretation of facts.

It is important to note that the validation of a possible mistake of fact in this context favors a finding of responsibility. The law would accept the error of the observer that the act was authorized by internal law or performed under a State's

[37] Ibid., para. 164.

[38] Ibid., para. 165.

[39] Ibid., paras. 166–169.

[40] Milanovic (2021).

[41] ILC (2001), Art. 7, para. 3 (emphasis added, footnotes removed).

effective control, but it would not give the same benefit to the mistake made by the State *organ* regarding the scope of her own competence[42] or the existence of an instruction or direction. In the context of Article 4 of the ILC's Articles, these notions emanate from the same basic rule: that international law does not take into account whether the act is lawful by the standards of internal law. The corollary is that the State cannot use that internal law to argue that the observer or the agent made a mistake that could invalidate the argument of responsibility. The same is arguably true for other grounds of attribution, but the international practice is scarce.

2.2.2 Error in Acknowledgement and Adoption

Under Article 11 of the Articles on State Responsibility, a State may become accountable for the non-attributable conduct of a third party if it acknowledges this conduct and adopts it as its own. This is a mechanism of attribution that operates *a posteriori*. Indeed, as the ILC says in its commentary, this provision does not assume that the agent fulfilled any of the other grounds of attribution at the time of the commission of the act.[43] The State as a legal person is entirely absent from the conduct in question.[44] It is the unilateral act of the State which, by recognizing the conduct and endorsing as its own, leads to the allocation of responsibility under international law.[45]

A corollary of the foregoing is that the act of acknowledgement and adoption is voluntary. In the author's view, it is best characterized as a unilateral act of the State, which is defined as an expression of will which emanates from the State and produces international legal effects.[46] It may well take the form of a declaration (a unilateral act *stricto sensu*)[47] or occur by virtue of non-verbal conduct,[48] as suggested by the *Lighthouses* arbitration,[49] or an accumulation of acts,[50] as was the case in *Tehran Hostages*.[51] Even the ILC's Guiding Principles Applicable to Unilateral Declarations of States Capable of Creating Legal Obligations, which govern only formal declarations,[52] acknowledge that States may find themselves bound by their unilateral behavior on the international plane, including what the ILC described as mere informal conduct, or even silence.[53] Acknowledgement and adoption under Article

[42] This would not be a mistake of law, since municipal law is a fact for international law.

[43] ILC (2001), Art. 11, para. 1.

[44] De Frouville (2010), pp. 273, 275.

[45] ILC (2001), Art. 11, para. 1.

[46] Rodríguez Cedeño and Torres Cazorla (2019), para. 13.

[47] Cf. ILC (2006), p. 368.

[48] Rodríguez Cedeño and Torres Cazorla (2019), para. 18.

[49] Cf. Arbitral Tribunal (1956), p. 197.

[50] ILC (2001), Art. 11, paras. 4–8.

[51] ICJ (1980), paras. 74, 31–33, 63–68.

[52] ILC (2006), p. 370, preamble and Guiding Principle 1.

[53] Ibid., p. 369.

11 of the ILC's Articles on State Responsibility is a singular example of a unilateral act. It is an act by which the State assumes responsibility for a non-attributable conduct, even retrospectively in appropriate cases.[54] The legal nature of the acknowledgement and adoption is revealed by the fact that, by taking up responsibility for the private conduct, the State is unilaterally assuming the obligation to abide by the dictates of the law of State responsibility, including, in principle, the obligation to make reparation, should the endorsed conduct be at variance with its obligations under international law.

The possible effect of a mistake of fact on the legal efficacy of a unilateral act depends on how one characterizes the legal nature of such an act. If one considers that the manifestation of will is an essential element of the unilateral act[55] (juridical act theory), then the mistake of fact that vitiates the foundations of that will could deprive the unilateral act of its legal effects. On the other hand, if the outward expression of will itself suffices, in whatever way it is manifested, and regardless of intent[56] (behavior theory), the psychological factor presupposed by the mistake of fact becomes legally irrelevant. In other words, the effects of a mistake of fact on the enforceability of the unilateral act of acknowledgement and adoption depend on the extent to which it is characterized as consensual, so that defects in the formation of consent could play a role in the determination of responsibility.

The answer to this theoretical question is not easy to find. As far as the ILC goes, the commentary to Article 11 of the Articles on State Responsibility does not answer this question conclusively. The closest reference may be the ILC's recognition that the scope of acknowledgement and adoption depends on the election of the endorsing State.[57] Seen in a broader perspective, it appears that the Guiding Principles on Unilateral Declarations have adopted an eclectic position.[58] The preamble highlights that, in practice, it is difficult to determine whether the unilateral act creates legal effects by virtue of the will that is expressed or the expectations that result from the conduct for other subjects of international law.[59] Some passages of the Guiding Principle give weight to the outward manifestation of will rather than its formation. For instance, the preamble refers to the binding legal effects that emanate from 'behaviors … on which other States may reasonably rely'.[60] When interpreting the scope of the unilateral undertakings, it is necessary to take into account all factual circumstances, including the 'reactions to which they gave rise'.[61]

It is worth reviewing the ICJ's jurisprudence regarding the interpretation of unilateral declarations accepting its jurisdiction under Article 36 (2) of the Statute, to which

[54] ILC (2001), Art. 11, para. 4 (noting that when the acknowledgement and adoption is unequivocal and unqualified, there may be good reason to treat it as retroactive).

[55] Rodríguez Cedeño and Torres Cazorla (2019), para. 1.

[56] Ibid.

[57] ILC (2001), Art. 11, para. 8.

[58] Rodríguez Cedeño and Torres Cazorla (2019), para. 1.

[59] ILC (2006), p. 369.

[60] Ibid.

[61] Ibid., Guiding Principles 3, 7.

the ILC's commentary refers as well.[62] Particularly, the ICJ has given importance to the intention of the declaring State when attributing meaning to a declaration (or reservation).[63] Indeed, the ICJ noted that 'since a declaration under Article 36, paragraph 2, of the Statute, is a unilaterally drafted instrument, the Court has not hesitated to place a certain emphasis on the intention of the depositing State'.[64] It should be noted, however, that this does not allow the Court to rely fully on the declared intention of that State, but rather to deduce it from objective manifestations to be found in the declaration and the circumstances of its making. In practice, this means drawing the analysis back to what is stated in the ILC's Guiding Principle 3. Therefore,

> The Court will thus interpret the relevant words of a declaration including a reservation contained therein in a natural and reasonable way, having due regard to the intention of the State concerned at the time when it accepted the compulsory jurisdiction of the Court. The intention of a reserving State may be deduced not only from the text of the relevant clause, but also from the context in which the clause is to be read, and an examination of evidence regarding the circumstances of its preparation and the purposes intended to be served.[65]

On the other hand, the Guiding Principles link the formation of unilateral declarations with that of treaties. In particular, when explaining why Guiding Principle 2 grants all States the capacity to issue binding unilateral declarations, the ILC directly references the international law of treaties and explains that 'Just as "(e)very State possesses capacity to conclude treaties", every State can commit itself through acts whereby it unilaterally undertakes legal obligations under the conditions indicated in these Guiding Principles'.[66] From this it may be deduced that the efficacy of the declaration is linked with consensual elements (bilateral or multilateral agreement in the case of treaties, and unilateral intent in the case of declarations).

The ILC also points to the Judgment handed down by the ICJ in the *Burkina Faso/ Mali* case where, in appraising the statement made by Mali's head of State on 11 April 1975, the Court recalled that declarations 'concerning legal or factual situations' may create legal obligations 'when it is the intention of the State making the declaration that it should become bound according to its terms'; hence, the declaration derives the 'character of a legal undertaking' from the intention of the State alone.[67] 'Thus it all depends on the intention of the State in question', the Court concluded.[68] Likewise, when interpreting Article 36 (2) of the Stature, as indicated above, the ICJ stated that the intention of the declaring State is an important factor to take into account. While this intent should be derived from objective manifestations, this does not mean that it is only the outward expression of the State that matters. Indeed, beyond simply looking at the text of the declaration, its context and the circumstances in which it

[62] Ibid., Guiding Principle 7, para. 3.

[63] ICJ (1998), para. 48.

[64] Ibid., para. 48.

[65] Ibid., para. 49.

[66] ILC (2006), p. 371.

[67] ICJ (1986b), para. 39.

[68] Ibid.

occurred, the ICJ has also given attention to 'the purposes intended to be served' by the declaration accepting jurisdiction and its reservations.[69] In that understanding, in the *Aegean Sea Continental Shelf* case, the ICJ asked the Greek Government to provide it with any available evidence of explanations of the instrument of accession given at the time of its making.[70] In *Fisheries Jurisdiction (Spain* v. *Canada)*, the Court looked at Canadian ministerial statements, parliamentary debates, legislative proposals and press communiqués to ascertain the meaning of the Canadian reservation.[71]

The author deduces from these considerations that the unilateral act derives its legal effects from *both* the will emanating from the State and the legitimate expectations it creates on other subjects of international law. Moreover, the regime of unilateral undertakings is supplemented by the law of treaties, where the analogy is possible. The answer to the relevance of mistakes of fact in instances of acknowledgement and adoption may lie at the intersection between these three factors.

As a starting point, the parallels between the regimes of unilateral undertakings and treaties are not infrequent. As mentioned before, the ILC deduces the capacity to assume obligations by unilateral declarations from the general treaty-making capacity of States under Article 6 of the Vienna Convention on the Law of Treaties.[72] Moreover, the ILC and the ICJ have found that there is a rule in this regime comparable to the one found in the law of treaties, according to which heads of State, heads of Government and ministers of foreign affairs are deemed to represent their State by their inherent functions and considered capable of binding the State, through treaties in the latter case, and through unilateral declarations in the case at hand.[73] The ILC also notes the ICJ's use of Article 31 (1) of the Vienna Convention by (limited) analogy to unilateral declarations accepting jurisdiction under Article 36 (2) of the ICJ Statute.[74] As for the nullifying effect of conflicts with *jus cogens*, the ILC explicitly states that 'The invalidity of a unilateral act which is contrary to a peremptory norm of international law derives from the analogous rule contained in article 53 of the 1969 Vienna Convention on the Law of Treaties.'[75] The ILC also applies Article 34 of the Vienna Convention by analogy to unilateral declarations, to conclude that such undertakings do not affect third States.[76] Finally, when substantiating the application of the theory of fundamental change of circumstances to unilateral declarations, the ILC directly subjects this rule to the 'strict limits' of the rule codified in Article 62 of the Vienna Convention.[77]

---

[69] ICJ (1998), para. 49.

[70] ICJ (1978), para. 69.

[71] ICJ (1998), para. 49.

[72] Ibid., Guiding Principle 2.

[73] Ibid., Guiding Principle 4, para. 1; see also ICJ (2006), para. 46 and the cases cited therein.

[74] Ibid., Guiding Principle 7, para. 3.

[75] Ibid., Guiding Principle 8, para. 1.

[76] Ibid., Guiding Principle 9, para. 1.

[77] Ibid., Guiding Principle 10, para. 3.

If one where to take these analogies to their logical conclusion, the argument would go that the Vienna Convention does contemplate error of fact under Article 48 (1) as a ground for invalidating consent to be bound by a treaty. Under this provision,

> A State may invoke an error in a treaty as invalidating its consent to be bound by the treaty if the error relates to a fact or situation which was assumed by that State to exist at the time when the treaty was concluded and formed an essential basis of its consent to be bound by the treaty.

Rensmann explains that under Article 48 it is the formation of consent rather than its expression that matters.[78] For the error to invalidate consent, it must bear a close relationship to the substance of the treaty, but not necessarily be reflected in the wording.[79] They must be errors as to the substance of the agreement (*error in substantia*) and not simply errors relating to the motivation to conclude it.[80] Thus, for example, in the *Kasikili/Sedudu Island* case, Judge Fleischhauer in his dissenting opinion considered that an error relating to the navigability of River Chobe did not invalidate the substance of the agreement between the United Kingdom and Germany inasmuch as it referred to the 'main channel' of that river as the dividing boundary between the territories of Botswana and Namibia.[81] Under Article 48 of the Vienna Convention, the fact or situation to which the error refers must have been an essential basis for the State's consent to be bound by the treaty. This may occur because the situation or fact was considered a condition for that consent, as was stated by the Permanent Court of International Justice in the *Mavrommatis Palestine Concessions* case.[82] In the end, the identification of an essential error of fact is objective, determined by the perspective of a third State in a similar situation.[83]

Article 48 (2) of the Vienna Convention clarifies that this invalidating ground does not apply if 'the State in question contributed by its own conduct to the error or if the circumstances were such as to put that State on notice of a possible error'. This provision excludes inexcusable errors.[84] Thus, Article 48 is capable of invalidating consent to be bound by a treaty if an essential element of such consent was based on an erroneous apprehension of the facts, so long as the error was excusable.

Following the ILC's treatment of the relationship between the regime of unilateral declarations and treaty law, a mistake of law that accumulates these elements would prevent any unilateral declaration from displaying its legal effects. The possibility of applying Article 48 of the Vienna Convention to unilateral declarations is revealed by the fact that the bilateral or multilateral character of the treaty or the obligations assumed under it does not play a pivotal role in the application of the concept of error. Indeed, according to the literature, Article 48 does not distinguish between unilateral and mutual errors.[85]

---

[78] Rensmann (2018), para. 14.

[79] Ibid., para. 15.

[80] Ibid., paras. 17, 18.

[81] Fleischhauer (1999), p. 1203, Rensmann (2018), para. 16.

[82] PCIJ (1924), pp. 30–31.

[83] Rensmann (2018), paras. 28, 29.

[84] Ibid., para. 31.

[85] Ibid., para. 12.

Nevertheless, to blindly transpose Article 48 to the law of unilateral acts would not fully address the underlying concerns outlined before. Indeed, the legitimate expectations created by a unilateral declaration play a pivotal role in demarcating the obligations assumed by the declaring State. This may be the reason why the ILC's Guiding Principles do not themselves transplant all the rules of treaty invalidity into the law of unilateral acts. In fact, the only ground of invalidity contemplated by the Guiding Principles is conflict with a peremptory rule of international law (jus cogens).[86] According to Rodríguez Cedeño and Torres Cazorla, this attitude indicates that the Guiding Principles preclude the consideration of other causes of nullity mentioned in the regime of the Vienna Convention on the Law of Treaties.[87] This reluctance is present in other areas: Reisman and Pulkowski point out, for example, the ICJ's apparent unwillingness to treat Article 36 (2) declarations accepting compulsory jurisdiction, or their reservations, as null and void.[88]

In the author's opinion, while this conclusion may contribute to preserving stability of unilateral commitments, it would forget that the Guiding Principles themselves do contemplate other grounds for the inefficacy of unilateral declarations, even if not under the name of nullity. Particularly, the Principles recognize that a unilateral declaration may be revoked.[89] The limit imposed is that the State cannot revoke a unilateral act arbitrarily.[90] To evaluate arbitrariness, the Guiding Principles refer to any terms in the declaration referring to revocation, the reliance by the beneficiaries of the unilateral act, and the extent to which there has been a fundamental change of circumstances.[91] Since this list is numerus apertus,[92] other considerations may be made, including, in the opinion of the author, the extent to which the will expressed through the unilateral act may have been vitiated by a circumstance prevailing at the time of the act's making. This would be in keeping with the nature of unilateral declarations as juridical acts. Indeed, the notion of arbitrariness is linked to good faith,[93] which itself allows consideration of defects of the formation of contractual will.[94] Moreover, considering the existence of a mistake of fact through the lens of Guiding Principle 10 has the benefit that the rule of arbitrariness allows the adjudicator to consider the crucial issue of reliance and estoppel,[95] and the extent to which the invocation of a mistake may be precluded by the terms of the declaration.[96] By using the notion of mistake found in Article 48, the adjudicator would also be in the position to gauge whether the error was excusable.

---

86 ILC (2006), Guiding Principle 8.

87 Rodríguez Cedeño and Torres Cazorla (2019), para. 28.

88 Reisman and Pulkowski (2006), para. 8.

89 ILC (2006), Guiding Principle 10.

90 Ibid., paras. 1–2.

91 Ibid., Guiding Principle 10 (a)–(c).

92 Ibid., para. 2.

93 Rodríguez Cedeño and Torres Cazorla (2019), para. 31.

94 Rensmann (2018), para. 1.

95 Ibid., para. 3.

96 Ibid., Guiding Principle 10 (a).

Understood this way, the regime applicable to Article 11 acknowledgements and adoptions would allow the State to revoke a prior declaration of endorsement invoking an excusable mistake of fact, thereby severing the link of responsibility. It is to be noted that, in light of the particular characteristics of this regime, a mistake of fact would only be capable of displaying these effects in rather exceptional cases. Most cases would concern an error of motivation rather than a genuine mistake of fact. Consider the case of a State that acknowledges and adopts the theft of a historical artifact of great cultural significance, only to later discover that the thief intended to destroy it. While the underlying facts may not have changed, the State's reasons behind the endorsement of the theft might have. This case, however, would not be covered by Article 48 of the Vienna Convention on the Law of Treaties, because it concerns the reasons behind the endorsement of the behavior and not the actual facts underlying it.

Perhaps an example of a genuine mistake of fact in this context would be a State adopting the theft of an artifact, believing that a completely different artifact had been stolen. If the identity of the artifact was an essential element behind the acknowledgement and adoption, the State may argue that this is a genuine instance of mistake of fact invalidating the subjective element behind its decision to adopt the conduct in question

References

De Frouville O (2010) Chapter 19.3. Attribution of conduct to the state: private individuals. In: Crawford J, Pellet A, Olleson S, Parlett K (eds) The law of international responsibility. Oxford University Press, pp 257–280

Milanovic M (2021) European Court Finds Russia Assassinated Alexander Litvinenko. https://www.ejiltalk.org/european-court-finds-russia-assassinated-alexander-litvinenko/. Accessed 9 Oct 2023

Reisman WM and Pulkowski D (2006) Nullity in international law. In: Max Planck Encyclopedia of Public International Law. Accessed 10 Mar 2024

Rensmann T (2018) Article 48. Error, 2nd edn. In: Dörr O, Schmalenbach K (eds) Vienna convention on the law of treaties: a commentary. Springer, pp 879–898

Rodríguez Cedeño V, Torres Cazorla MI (2019) Unilateral acts of States in international law. In: Max Planck Encyclopedia of Public International Law. Accessed 10 Mar 2024

Schwenzer I, Hachem P, Kee C (2012) Global sales and contract law. Oxford University Press

Smith S (2004) Theory of contract. Oxford University Press

Case Law and Related Documents

Arbitral Tribunal (1956) Affaire relative à la concession des phares de l'Empire ottoman (Grèce, France) (24/27 July 1956). RIAA Vol XII:155-269

ECtHR (2021) Case of Carter *v.* Russia. Judgment (21 Sept 2021). App no 20914/07

Fleischhauser J (1999) Dissenting opinion. In: ICJ, case concerning Kasikili/Sedudu Island (Botswana/Namibia). Judgment. ICJ Rep 1999:1045, pp 1196–1207

ICJ (1978) Aegean Sea Continental Shelf (Greece *v.* Turkey). Judgment. ICJ Rep 1978:3
ICJ (1980) United States Diplomatic and Consular Staff in Tehran (United States of America *v.* Iran). Judgment. ICJ Rep 1980:3
ICJ (1986a) Case concerning military and paramilitary activities in and against Nicaragua (Nicaragua *v.* United States of America). Judgment. ICJ Rep 1986:14
ICJ (1986b) Case concerning the frontier dispute (Burkina Faso/Republic of Mali). Judgment. ICJ Rep 1986:554
ICJ (1998) Fisheries jurisdiction (Spain *v.* Canada). Judgment. ICJ Rep 1998:432
ICJ (2006) Armed activities on the territory of the Congo (new application: 2002) (Democratic Republic of the Congo *v.* Rwanda). Judgment. ICJ Rep 2006:6
ICJ (2007) Case concerning application of the convention on the prevention and punishment of the crime of genocide (Bosnia and Herzegovina *v.* Serbia and Montenegro). Judgment. ICJ Rep 2007:43
PCIJ (1924) The Mavrommatis Palestine concessions. Judgment. Series A no 2

International Law Commission (ILC) documents

Ago (1972) Fourth report on state responsibility by Mr. Roberto Ago, special rapporteur—the internationally wrongful act of the state, source of international responsibility. ILC Yearbook 1979, vol II Part 1
ILC (1972) ILC Yearbook 1972, vol II
ILC (1975) ILC Yearbook 1975, vol II
ILC (2001) Draft articles on the responsibility of states for internationally wrongful acts, with commentaries thereto. ILC Yearbook 2001, vol II Part Two
ILC (2006) Guiding principles applicable to unilateral declarations of states capable of creating legal obligations, with commentaries thereto. ILC Yearbook 2006, vol II Part Two

Legal Instruments

Articles on the responsibility of states for internationally wrongful acts. ILC Yearbook 2001, vol II Part Two [articles on state responsibility]
Draft articles on the responsibility of international organizations. ILC Yearbook 2011, vol II Part Two [draft articles on the responsibility of international organizations]
Vienna Convention on the Law of Treaties. 25 May 1969. UNTS 1155:331

Chapter 3
Mistake of Fact in the Establishment of a Breach

3.1 Finding Fault

Once attribution has been established, the time comes to determine whether the conduct in question conflicts with an international obligation of the State. In other words, it is the moment to determine whether a *breach* has occurred. In that sense, our inquiry should lead us to questioning whether a mistake of fact can prevent this from happening. This should immediately bring back the concern as to whether international responsibility is *objective* or strict (in which case the mistake of fact would be inoperative) or whether it is *subjective* or based on fault or blameworthiness (in which case a genuine, excusable and reasonable mistake of fact may prevent a breach from being established).

The answer to this question lies in the structure of the rules on international responsibility as codified in the ILC's Articles. During codification, an attempt was made to distinguish between primary and secondary rules, the first set governing the content of the substantive obligation, and the second describing the legal implications of its breach.[1] The rules on State responsibility belong to the second category.[2] While the content of the primary rule would change depending on the applicable international law, it is understood that the rules describing international responsibility, as secondary norms, would apply across the board except where a *lex specialis* exists.[3] Thus, to decide if a mistake of fact can be considered a 'general' ground to excuse non-performance of an international obligation, one must look to the rules of State responsibility as they exist in customary international law.

Yet, Articles 2 and 12–15 of the Articles on State Responsibility do not provide a clear answer. Article 2 simply describes the need for the conduct to 'constitut[e] a breach of an international obligation of the State'. Article 12 laconically states that a

[1] ILC (2001), General Commentary, paras. 1–4.

[2] Ibid., paras. 1, 3.

[3] Article 55 of the Articles on State Responsibility.

J. P. Hernández Páez, *Mistake of Fact in Public International Law*,
SpringerBriefs in Law, https://doi.org/10.1007/978-3-031-59508-0_3

breach exists when 'an act of that State is not in conformity with what is required of it by that obligation'. Article 13 specifies that the obligation must be in force for the State at the time of the conduct. Article 14 regulates continuing breaches, and Article 15 describes the concept of a composite wrongful act. No straightforward answers are to be found in the black-letter text of the Articles on State Responsibility. The commentary, however, explains why this attitude prevails in the Articles. In analyzing the notion of attribution adopted in the Articles, the commentary to Article 2 explains the following:

> Whether there has been a breach of a rule may depend on the intention or knowledge of relevant State organs or agents and in that sense may be "subjective". For example, article II of the Convention on the Prevention and Punishment of the Crime of Genocide states that: "In the present Convention, genocide means any of the following acts committed with intent to destroy, in whole or in part, a national, ethnical, racial or religious group, as such ..." In other cases, the standard for breach of an obligation may be "objective", in the sense that the advertence or otherwise of relevant State organs or agents may be irrelevant. *Whether responsibility is "objective" or "subjective" in this sense depends on the circumstances, including the content of the primary obligation in question. The articles lay down no general rule in that regard.* The same is true of other standards, whether they involve some degree of fault, culpability, negligence or want of due diligence. Such standards vary from one context to another for reasons which essentially relate to the object and purpose of the treaty provision or other rule giving rise to the primary obligation. Nor do the articles lay down any presumption in this regard as between the different possible standards. Establishing these is a matter for the interpretation and application of the primary rules engaged in the given case.[4]

This excerpt of the commentary might lead the reader to the conclusion that the Articles on State Responsibility do not adopt a theory at all. Indeed, whether an obligation is objective or subjective is a question that is best answered by the primary norm. The secondary norms on responsibility, intended to apply generally, are not in the position to draw this line and any other conclusion risks blurring the line between the primary and secondary regimes.

At the same time, it is unclear what happens when the objective or subjective character of the primary obligation is not evident. Following the ILC's reasoning, this would surely be an issue of interpretation. Yet, the Articles on State Responsibility endeavor to provide an answer just a few paragraphs later, still within the commentary to Article 2:

> A related question is whether fault constitutes a necessary element of the internationally wrongful act of a State. This is certainly not the case if by "fault" one understands the existence, for example, of an intention to harm. *In the absence of any specific requirement of a mental element in terms of the primary obligation, it is only the act of a State that matters, independently of any intention.*[5]

Thus, if the primary rule is not 'subjective' in its terms, the fallback presumption would be that responsibility is objective or strict, and considerations of the intention behind the wrongful conduct do not play a role. The juxtaposition of these two

---

[4] ILC (2001), Art. 2, para. 3 (emphasis added).

[5] Ibid., para. 10 (emphasis added).

paragraphs within the same commentary is quite puzzling. As Koskenniemi puts it, it is difficult to identify whether, by rejecting a general requirement of fault, the Articles on State Responsibility are attempting to define an abstract presumption of objective or strict responsibility or, rather, they are simply referring to the primary norm's content.[6] While part of the commentary to Article 2 seems to favor the theory that the Articles opt for a *renvoi* in favor of the primary legal regime, the standard of Article 12 requiring objective non-conformity between the act and the obligation, understood in the content of the other passages of the commentary to Article 2 would point in a different direction. Indeed, the question whether State responsibility requires fault or blameworthiness (*culpa*) is still considered by some authors to be somewhat debatable, although generally leaning in favor of objective responsibility.[7]

From a practical and political perspective, objective responsibility certainly accords better with the realities of international life. It provides for the straightforward rule that any action that causes injury to a legal right must be compensated, a rule that is consistent with diplomatic practice and ensures regular and peaceful relations between States.[8] It is also complex in practice for analyses of fault or blameworthiness to be transposed from an individual actor to a State. Indeed, a juristic entity cannot in principle be subjectively blameworthy (*societas delinquere non potest*).[9] The rule of objective responsibility allocates responsibility in a better and more economical way because it assigns the risk of breach to the entity that performs the act, and not the injured party, who would be required to investigate the wrongdoer's state of mind at the time of the breach. On the other hand, even if complicated in practice, assigning subjective blameworthiness to a State is not implausible, as it is always practicable to investigate a series of factors, including the degree of fault of the State agent and whether the limits of that agent's competence have been drawn adequately by the State. Conversely, according to some authors, the fault-based theory of State responsibility would have the policy advantage of forcing the State to be conscious of its international duties,[10] although this is a position that rings truer when it comes to mistake of *law* analyses rather than the ones we have at hand. Looking at the intricate interplay between these legal and political considerations, it stands to reason why the ILC decided to step back and leave this mess for the primary norms to decide.

What flows from the ILC's commentary to Article 2 of the Articles on State Responsibility and the relevant international practice is that the State's accountability is primarily objective, unless the obligation at bar requires a particular mental state. Since all that is required is the strict lack of conformity between the State's conduct and the obligation incumbent on it under international law, the necessary conclusion is that mistakes of fact generally have no legal effect insofar as one is addressing the

[6] Koskenniemi (2010), p. 50.

[7] Cf. Shaw (2017), p. 593.

[8] Pellet (2010), p. 6.

[9] Ibid.

[10] Lauterpacht (1927), p. 140.

concept of 'breach'. Thus, the efficacy of a mistake of fact in any individual case will depend on the primary rule. If the obligation requires a specific mental state, the mistake will display its legal effects only if it can remove that intentional or volitional element in the individual facts of the case.

It is important to mention that some factors involved in this analysis may not directly impact the notion of 'breach' as much as they would other elements of responsibility. For instance, in cases involving putative self-defense or mistaken countermeasures,[11] what is at stake is not whether a 'breach' has occurred in the sense of Article 2 of the Articles on State Responsibility, but rather whether the wrongfulness of the breach can be *precluded* on another basis. This other aspect will not be addressed in this chapter.

3.2 Case Studies

3.2.1 Shootdown of Civil Aircraft

One of the most paradigmatic examples of alleged wrongful acts committed by mistake is perhaps the use of force against civilian airplanes incorrectly believed to constitute military threats. The examples are simply too numerous. Our analysis needs to start with the very provision that governs (*rectius*, prohibits) the use of weapons against civilian aircraft in the first place. Article 3 *bis* (*a*) of the Chicago Convention on International Civil Aviation provides as follows:

> The contracting States recognize that every State must refrain from resorting to the use of weapons against civil aircraft in flight and that, in case of interception, the lives of persons on board and the safety of aircraft must not be endangered. This provision shall not be interpreted as modifying in any way the rights and obligations of States set forth in the Charter of the United Nations.

At the time this provision was negotiated and incorporated in the Chicago Convention, the crux of the debate concerned whether States' sovereignty over their respective airspaces gave them the right to resort to the use of force (including overwhelming or lethal force) against so-called civil aerial intruders, i.e. civil aircraft that entered the airspace of another State without clearance or authorization. As Augustin frames it, the key question was whether the principle of complete and exclusive sovereignty over airspace granted a State whose airspace had been violated boundless discretion to respond to the intrusion.[12]

According to Augustin, some standards can be distilled from the State practice regarding aerial intruders prior to the adoption of Article 3 *bis*. The use of force was only exceptionally permitted by customary international law; States were duty-bound to exert all reasonable efforts to identify the intruder; civil aircraft intruding due to

---

[11] See Chap. 4.

[12] Augustin (1998), p. 13.

mistake or force majeure had to be treated more leniently and afforded assistance[13]; force could not be used against civil aerial intruders even if they disobeyed the orders of the territorial State, unless they posed or appeared to pose a threat to the security of that State, in which case necessary and proportionate force could be exerted, in line with considerations of humanity.[14] All too often, States claimed that the victim had not been identified as a civilian aircraft, or that it was reasonably believed to be a military threat.[15]

Thus, the rules of customary international law prior to Article 3 *bis* were more lenient regarding the use of force against civilian aircraft in cases of aerial intrusions.[16] While force was discouraged and subject to legal restraints, it appears that States could still use it in a manner necessary and proportionate, not only in respect of *actual* threats to State security, but also in response to *perceived* threats. At the time, then, a reasonable mistake of fact followed by a necessary and proportionate response could *ex hypothesi* be justifiable under international law on that basis. This could permit anywhere from a more clement interception by the territorial State to force the intruder to land or change course, to actual use of weapons to avert a threat believed to be directed against the security in that State. And indeed, the record shows that this was sometimes the case.

However, the position at customary international law started to change in the decades following the Second World War. The changes started to show after the El Al Israeli Airlines incident. On 27 July 1955 Bulgaria shot down an Israeli airliner that was allegedly flying through its airspace without clearance. Israel condemned this action and presented a draft resolution to the United Nations General Assembly dealing with the question of the safety of commercial aircraft flying in the vicinity of, or inadvertently crossing, international frontiers. On 14 December 1955, the General Assembly adopted resolution 927 (X), in which it noted that

> ...[I]ncidents involving attacks on civil aircraft innocently deviating from fixed plans in the vicinity of, or across, international frontiers ... cause loss of human life and affect relations between States, and ... the problem is therefore a matter of general international concern...

and called upon all States to 'take the necessary measures to avoid such incidents', calling this situation to the attention of the 'appropriate international organizations'.[17]

In response to this resolution, the Secretary General of the International Civil Aviation Organization (ICAO) issued a working paper addressing the legal and technical aspects of these incidents. It noted that the laws of many States permitted the use of weapons against aerial intruders when they crossed into their airspace without

---

[13] See Chap. 4 on the issue of mistaken aerial intrusions and the relevance of force majeure.

[14] Augustin (1998), pp. 46–47.

[15] Ibid., p. 48 (emphasis added).

[16] It is to be noted that these considerations may only apply to the internal use of force against aerial intruders within a State's own territory. The extraterritorial use of force remained subject to the peremptory limits set by the United Nations Charter and relevant rules of customary law. Augustin himself points out the consensus at international law that in such cases, the Charter may not be applicable at all. See Augustin (1998), pp. 26–27.

[17] A/RES/927(X), preamble and paras. 1, 2.

air traffic control clearance, deviated from air corridors or entered into prohibited areas.[18]

> Also, the assertion has been made by some Governments that it is contrary to international law for a State to shoot down a civil, unarmed aircraft *under any circumstances*, (there being no question of repelling an attack), while, on the other hand, this principle has been denied by some States...[19]

In response to a later working paper by the ICAO Air Navigation Committee alerting to the difficulty of defining universally applicable signals and procedures for interception in cases of aerial intrusion,[20] the ICAO Secretary General conducted a new survey of national practice and law and identified the need to develop new rules to prevent these incidents from reoccurring. Going beyond the language of General Assembly resolution 927 (X), it was suggested that any such rules should not only cover flights in the vicinity or crossing international frontiers without clearance, but also incidents of authorized entry where aircraft innocently deviate from course and cross into prohibited areas.[21] It distinguished these cases, where 'merely ... aerial sovereignty was violated' from instances where self-defense may be required.[22] At this time, however, referring the matter to the Legal Committee for consideration was not accepted by the ICAO Council despite the Secretary General's recommendation.[23]

This decision notwithstanding, and even though this incident did not yet lead to a complete paradigm shift in customary international law, the cracks had already started to show. In 1957, Israel, the United States and the United Kingdom brought separate ICJ proceedings against Bulgaria regarding the aerial incident of 27 July 1955. Some of the claims went as follows.

In the United States Memorial, it was pointed out that this incident had not been a case of mere mistake or negligence.[24] Instead, the United States claim was that Bulgaria had willfully and intentionally attacked the civilian airliner, and consequently violated international law by killing United States nationals. Moreover, it made the interesting argument that Bulgaria was under an international, 'affirmative' duty to succor, rather than to attack, the straying plane. It grounded this duty on maritime law precedents,[25] and comparing them to the law of the air as codified in the Brussels Conventions of 1910 and 1938,[26] as well as prior aerial incidents involving unarmed transport.[27] Though perhaps not explicitly, the United States would appear

---

[18] C-WP/2153, para. 5.

[19] Ibid., para. 5 (emphasis added).

[20] See C-WP/2376.

[21] C-WP/2609, paras. 15–23.

[22] Ibid., paras. 15–23.

[23] ICAO Doc 7985-C/908, para. 16.

[24] United States (1958), p. 229.

[25] Ibid., pp. 216–221.

[26] Ibid., pp. 221 ff.

[27] Ibid., pp. 225 ff.

to have been referring to a duty under customary international law to render assistance to an aircraft in distress.

For its part, the United Kingdom relied on the ICJ's *Corfu Channel* case, arguing that 'international law condemns actions by States which in time of peace unnecessarily or recklessly involve risk to the lives of the nationals of other States or destruction of their property.'[28] Analogizing from the position under the international law of the sea, the United Kingdom pointed out that 'international law, on grounds of humanity, recognizes for ships a right of entry into the territory of a foreign State in cases of overriding necessity'.[29] It also referred to some aerial incidents, including the shootdown of a United States aircraft by Yugoslavia in 1946 to buttress this position, showing that, although the Yugoslavian authorities only accepted granting compensation *ex gratia* and without admitting legal liability, orders were given to military authorities not to shoot upon unauthorized aircraft but rather to invite them to land.[30]

Finally, the Israeli Memorial grounded Bulgaria's responsibility on customary international law.[31] Israel argued that the force employed by Bulgaria against the airliner was clearly 'out of proportion' to the threat that the plane could have posed[32]:

> The basis of this contention is the rule that when measures of force are employed to protect territorial sovereignty, whether on land, on sea or in the air, their employment is subject to the duty to take into consideration the elementary obligations of humanity, and not to use a degree of force in excess of what is commensurate with the reality and the gravity of the threat (if any).[33]

Israel relied on *Corfu Channel* to make this point.[34] While accepting that in extreme cases, Bulgaria was entitled under international law to protect its sovereignty, including through self-defense,

> There is obviously considerable difference between operating a scheduled international air service over or into Bulgaria, and innocently overflying a stretch of Bulgarian territory. This type of infringement of territorial airspace is not uncommon, and at times may be unavoidable. It ought never to he opposed by such a disproportionate degree of violence as was employed in this case.[35]

Unfortunately, the ICJ never ruled on the merits of the case because it considered itself lacking jurisdiction to proceed with Israel's suit,[36] and the United States and the United Kingdom opted to discontinue their own applications.

The slow but steady change in customary international law is shown by an additional incident. On 21 February 1973, Libyan Arab Airlines Boeing 727 was shot

---

[28] United Kingdom (1958), para. 67.

[29] Ibid., para. 68.

[30] Ibid., para. 77.

[31] Israel (1958), para. 59.

[32] Ibid., para. 60.

[33] Ibid., para. 61.

[34] Ibid., para. 62.

[35] Ibid., para. 65.

[36] ICJ (1959), p. 147.

down by Israel for flying into a prohibited military zone. This time, instead of requesting States to 'avoid' aerial incidents of this kind, the ICAO Assembly and Council both condemned the use of force as a 'flagrant violation of the principles in the Chicago Convention'.[37]

The tipping point was the Korean Airlines Boeing 747 (Flight KE 007) incident, occurring on the night of 31 August 1978. The aircraft had strayed from its path into a prohibited military zone in the Soviet Union, which in turn shot it down. This, again, was not an instance of mistake of fact. However, the statements by countries following the incident are helpful in that respect. When requesting the President of the United Nations Security Council to convene an urgent meeting, the United States declared that the Soviet Union's actions violated 'fundamental legal norms and standards of international civil aviation' and that, crucially, '[t]here exists *no justification in international law for the destruction of an identifiable civil aircraft*.'[38] The Republic of Korea called the act 'barbaric' and 'unprovoked'. Agreeing with the United States position, the Republic of Korea claimed during the ensuing Security Council meeting that '*no provision of international law* … justifies the use of force against an unarmed civilian airliner *under any circumstances*'.[39] Canada called it a 'flagrant' and 'unacceptable' violation of international law. Australia flagged it as 'incompatible with civilized behavior between States' and agreed that there was '*no circumstance* in which *any nation* can be justified in shooting down an unarmed civilian aircraft serving no military purpose.'[40] Togo said that there was 'no provision' in the Chicago Convention authorizing a State to destroy a civil aircraft when it strayed into its airspace without authorization.[41]

For its part, the ICAO Council was seized of the matter in September 1983. It declared that the Soviet Union's actions had infringed the Chicago Convention and international law generally and directed the Air Navigation Committee to review the provisions of the Convention, including the possibility of the amendments necessary to prevent this tragedy from reoccurring.[42] The ICAO Assembly endorsed the Council's resolutions.[43] On 6 March 1984, the ICAO Council adopted a new resolution calling upon ICAO Members to 'cooperate fully in the work of examining and adopting an amendment to the Chicago Convention … and in the improvement of measures for preventing a recurrence of this type of tragedy…'.[44] On 10 May 1984, the ICAO Assembly adopted the Montreal Protocol amending the Chicago Convention to add Article 3 *bis* as it stands today.

The text of Article 3 *bis* does not directly address the issue of mistakes of fact in the shootdown of civilian aircraft believed to constitute military threats. However, two

[37] See Resolution A19-1, ICAO Doc 9124; ICAO Doc 9097-C/1016.

[38] Augustin (1998), p. 37 (emphasis added).

[39] Emphasis added.

[40] Augustin (1998), pp. 37, 38 (emphasis added).

[41] Ibid., p. 39.

[42] ICAO Doc 9416-C/1077.

[43] See Resolution A24-5, ICAO Doc 9414.

[44] ICAO Doc 9441-C/1081.

factors are important. First, the language of Article 3 *bis* is clear and unequivocal: it recognizes that such actions are not compatible with international law. It is categorical insofar as it relates to unarmed civilian aircraft. This supports the conclusion that under this provision a mistake of fact does not exonerate a State that has shot down a passenger aircraft. Second, the only carve-out found in Article 3 *bis* is the reference at the end to the rights of States under the United Nations Charter. This should be understood as a reference to the inherent right of States to individual or collective self-defense under Article 51 of the Charter.[45] These two interpretative factors taken together show that the use of weapons against a civilian aircraft, even under the influence of a mistake of fact, always constitutes a 'breach'[46] of Article 3 *bis* (*a*). The facts leading up to the adoption of this article, as detailed in this section, also confirm this: the accumulating *opinio juris* of States at the time was, clearly, that an unarmed civilian aircraft should never be shot upon, much less shot down, under *any* circumstances. In other words, there is no excuse or justification under international law for the use of weapons against an unarmed civil aircraft in flight.

The author now turns to State practice following the adoption of Article 3 *bis* of the Chicago Convention, which buttresses these conclusions under the Convention itself, related instruments and customary international law.

Perhaps the most commonly cited post-Article 3 *bis* case is the shootdown of Iran Air Flight 655, a passenger flight that was scheduled to travel from Tehran to Dubai. On 3 July 1988, before it could complete its habitual route, the civilian aircraft was shot down while flying over the Persian Gulf by the USS *Vincennes*, a United States navy cruiser using surface-to-air missiles. It is reported that all passengers were killed by the strike. The explanation given by the United States Government was that the Navy cruiser had misidentified the Airbus A300 as a F-14 Tomcat operated by the Iranian military. Thus, the United States insisted that the shootdown, although regrettable, had been orchestrated in self-defense. While the merits of this self-defense argument will be analyzed in a subsequent chapter, it is worth pointing out that the United States did not formally admit legal liability in respect of the aerial incident, although it did acknowledge the scale of the human tragedy caused by the shootdown.

In response to the United States' insistence that the shootdown, though lamentable, was in conformity with international law, Iran brough the case to the ICJ. In its Memorial in the *Aerial Incident of 3 July 1988* case,[47] Iran divided its arguments as to the shootdown of Flight 655 into two parts. The second challenged the United States argument that the use of force had been in accordance with the law of self-defense and will not be addressed here. The first part is directly relevant to the present inquiry, since Iran delved into the question whether the United States argument based on a mistake of fact (the so-called 'accidental' argument) was tenable under international law.

Iran framed the legal analysis in the following terms:

---

[45] See Chap. 4.

[46] See Articles 2 and 12 of the Articles on State Responsibility.

[47] See Iran (1990), 238 ff.

> ...the record shows that the Commanding Officer meant to shoot down the plane that appeared on his ship's radar. The question is rather *whether there was a mistaken identification of the plane and, if so, whether that mistaken identification justified in some way the shooting down of the plane or exonerated the United States from legal responsibility.*[48]

The first step taken by Iran was to dispel the notion that the USS *Vincennes* had erred in its identification of the civil aircraft. Iran pointed out *inter alia* that the USS *Vincennes* had the technical capacity to identify civilian aircraft[49]; the aircraft was squawking its commercial Mode III throughout the flight, which was a civilian frequency, and it was flying well within ATS route A59, its designated international air corridor; and the United States was aware of the flight schedules showing the Iran Air Flight 655 flying through that route at the relevant time.[50] Even if it had in fact been an F-14 Tomcat, Iran indicated that its military craft had avoided the United States naval forces since 1984 and that in any case an F-14 would have been incapable of the type of aerial attack feared by the USS *Vincennes*.[51]

In a second step, accepting *arguendo* that the mistake could have been made, Iran turned to the argument that the United States would be internationally responsible either way. Interestingly, Iran started by comparing the situation to municipal law. Given the paucity of materials dealing with this question, this comparison is understandable:

> In municipal law, the only difference between murder and manslaughter is that in order to prove the latter *there is no need to show an intention to kill*, but only an unlawful act which resulted in death. Here, *the unlawfulness of the act can be established on the objective facts*: either the shooting down of IR 655 was intentional or it was grossly negligent and reckless. In either case, the United States actions still have the character of an international crime and the United States bears full responsibility.[52]

In any case, 'the mistaken identification of the plane as an F-14 would not have made the act of shooting it down any less unlawful',[53] because, even if it had in fact been an F-14 instead of a civil aircraft, the United States would not have been legally entitled to shoot it down anyway.[54] Iran concludes by pointing out that 'the test of a State's responsibility is very wide', citing Brownlie in support of the proposition that State responsibility is objective,[55] and the *Kling* case[56] to show that '[i]n cases

---

[48] Ibid., para. 4.48 (emphasis added).

[49] Ibid., paras. 4.49, 4.50.

[50] Ibid., para. 4.50.

[51] Ibid., para. 4.50.

[52] Ibid., para. 4.53 (emphasis added).

[53] Ibid., para. 4.54 (emphasis removed).

[54] This part of Iran's argument appears to suggest that any 'mistake of fact' defense raised by the United States would require the mistake to be material in some way. Since the action would have been unlawful even if the mistake had actually been made and was reasonable, then the defense fails. This conclusion needs to be compared to Iran's immediate argument that international responsibility is objective anyway; thus, the mistake is wholly irrelevant.

[55] Iran (1990), para. 4.55.

[56] The *Kling* case as well as others similar to it will be addressed in Sect. 3.2.2 of this chapter.

of this kind it is mistaken action ... for which a government in a given case has been held responsible. The international precedents reveal the application of principles as to the very strict accountability for mistaken action.'[57] Thus, 'it makes no difference whether other crew members passed on wrong information: the United States would be liable for the destruction of IR 655 even if it resulted from mistaken actions.'[58]

Unfortunately, the case of Iran Air Flight 655 never resulted in a Judgment by the ICJ that could rule authoritatively on the question of mistakes of fact, at least in the context of air law. The United States and Iran reached a settlement according to which the United States would pay compensation *ex gratia* and without admitting legal responsibility.[59] However, this case provides valuable State practice as to how international responsibility may be interpreted. It also provides some insight as to States' understanding of self-defense in these situations.[60] At least from Iran's perspective, international responsibility is objective. Thus, mistakes of fact are entirely irrelevant for the question whether the shootdown of Iran Air Flight 655 was an internationally wrongful act.

At the same time, it is hard to argue that this basic position as to the conceptualization of State responsibility was denied *per se* by the United States. Of course, any consideration of the United States position needs to be taken with a cubic meter of salt, since the Respondent's arguments in the *Aerial Incident of 3 July 1988* case concerned only the question of ICJ jurisdiction, which the United States denied in the specific case. If one interprets the position taken by the United States elsewhere from a legal standpoint, one can draw very interesting conclusions. The United States argument was, essentially, that the USS *Vincennes* acted in (putative) self-defense, believing that the aircraft was, in fact, an F-14 engaged in hostile action against the Navy cruiser. Of course, if this self-defense argument were to be accepted, then the shootdown would have been in accordance with the international law on the use of force. Taking this argument at its best, by resorting to self-defense (a circumstance precluding wrongfulness[61] and an exception to the prohibition on the use of force[62]), the United States is accepting, *in principle*, that the use of force against Iran Air Flight 655 would have been at variance with international law, had the cruiser not acted in self-defense. Since the establishment and preclusion of wrongfulness are two separate concepts, this would lead to the conclusion that both States agreed that the claimed mistake of fact would not have prevented the Court from finding that an internationally wrongful act had occurred. Whether the mistake would have exonerated the United States by *precluding* the wrongfulness of the shootdown, is a separate question. This inference is in line with the ICJ's own case law. As the Court stated in *Nicaragua*,

---

57 ICJ (1990), para. 4.56.

58 Ibid., para. 4.56.

59 See Rajaee (1993).

60 See Chap. 4.

61 See Article 21 of the Articles on State Responsibility.

62 See Article 51 of the United Nations Charter.

> The Court would observe that the normal purpose of an invocation of self-defence is to justify conduct which would otherwise be wrongful. If advanced as a justification in itself, not coupled with a denial of the conduct alleged, it may well imply both an admission of that conduct, and of the wrongfulness of that conduct in the absence of the justification of self-defence. This reasoning would do away with any difficulty in establishing the facts, which would have been the subject of an implicit overall admission by the United States, simply through its attempt to justify them by the right of self-defence...[63]

Similarly, in the context of the identification of customary international law, the ICJ explained in the same case that '[i]f a State acts in a way *prima facie* incompatible with a recognized rule, but defends its conduct by appealing to exceptions or justifications contained within the rule itself, then whether or not the State's conduct is justifiable on that basis, the significance of that attitude is to confirm rather than to weaken the rule.'[64]

A second case that provides insight into this question is the claim brought by Ukraine against the Russian Federation before the ICJ in 2017. Ukraine claimed that the Russian Federation's support for armed insurrection in Eastern Ukraine constituted financing of terrorism in violation of the International Convention for the Suppression of the Financing of Terrorism (ICSFT) and that its harassment and discrimination of the Ukrainian people in the Autonomous Republic of Crimea and the city of Sevastopol, illegally annexed by Russia in 2014, violated the International Convention on the Elimination of All Forms of Racial Discrimination (CERD). A pivotal part of this dispute concerned the shootdown of Malaysian Airlines Flight MH17, which caused the death of 298 people on board.[65]

In its Counter-Memorial, the Russian Federation made a number of interesting observations in assessing whether the shootdown of Malaysian Airways Flight MH17 constituted an act of terrorism that could trigger Article 2 (1) (*a*) of the ICSFT. According to this provision, a terrorist act is '[a]n act which constitutes an offence within the scope of and as defined in one of the treaties in the annex', including the Montreal Convention on the Suppression of Unlawful Acts against the Safety of Civil Aviation. Russia argued that the shootdown of MH17 did not trigger Article 1 (1) (*b*) of the Montreal Convention, which criminalizes the act of intentionally 'destroy[ing] an aircraft in service or caus[ing] damage to such an aircraft which renders it incapable of flight or which is likely to endanger its safety in flight'. In the Russian Federation's position, the term 'aircraft in service' necessarily refers to civil aircraft and excludes military planes.[66] Then, Russia considered whether a mere *belief* that MH17 constituted a military aircraft could exclude it from the Montreal Convention's protections according to State practice. In other words, '[i]t is also instructive to consider whether other episodes involving the destruction of

---

[63] ICJ (1986), para. 74.

[64] Ibid., para. 186 (italics in the original).

[65] Ukraine (2018), para. 9.

[66] Russian Federation (2021), paras. 157–162.

civil aircraft in error have been alleged to constitute (or have been prosecuted as) a breach of Article 1(1)(b) (or the relevant offence as implemented in domestic law).'[67]

Of course, MH17 was indisputably a civilian aircraft. Russia's argument then is fundamentally a contention based on the theory of mistake of fact. To substantiate this argument, Russia referred to the shootdown of Ukrainian International Airlines Flight 752 in 2020 by Iran, which had mistaken it for an enemy cruise missile.[68] According to Russia, States did not characterize this as a breach of Article 1 (1) (*b*) of the Montreal Convention but instead as simply a regrettable tragedy.[69] This argument is flawed because, as will be explained later, this shootdown was the object of another international claim before the ICJ, filed by Ukraine, Canada, Sweden and the United Kingdom. Russia also referred to the alleged shootdown of Flight 1812 by Ukraine over the Black Sea in 2001, in response to which 'Russia neither characterized this as a terrorist act nor invoked Article 1(1)(b) of the Montreal Convention.'[70]

In response to this argument, Ukraine pointed out that the Russian Federation did not contest that the Donetsk People's Republic (DPR) forces intended to destroy an aircraft, and that they had no legal justification to do so.[71] Rather, as Ukraine characterized it, the Russian Federation's argument was that 'the attackers had hoped to shoot down a military aircraft, not a civilian one.'[72] According to Ukraine, this was irrelevant because there is no requirement in the Montreal Convention for the intention to shoot down a *civilian* aircraft to be proven; it sufficed that they intended to shoot down an aircraft, and that the aircraft was civilian in character.[73]

> Thus, any claim that the DPR intended to destroy a military aircraft instead of a civilian aircraft is not a defense. The Montreal Convention violation is established by the undisputed facts: that the DPR intended to destroy an aircraft; its actions were unlawful; and those actions did in fact destroy a civilian aircraft.[74]

Moreover, even if this intention was required, Ukraine considered that it was established on the facts, since firing into civilian airspace using a weapon incapable of distinguishing between civilian and military targets was enough to violate Article 1 (1) (*b*) of the Montreal Convention.[75]

In its Rejoinder, the Russian Federation doubled down on the mistake argument. Its position was that 'error obviously cannot be qualified as terrorism.'[76] It reiterated the argument that the intention to destroy a military aircraft during an ongoing armed conflict was not covered by the Montreal Convention.[77]

---

[67] Ibid., para. 163.

[68] Ibid., para. 164.

[69] Ibid.

[70] Ibid.

[71] Ukraine (2022), para. 203.

[72] Ibid., para. 204.

[73] Ibid., para. 205.

[74] Ibid.

[75] Ibid., para. 206.

[76] Russian Federation (2023), para. 237.

[77] Ibid., para. 242.

Interestingly, this Rejoinder includes legal analysis that clarifies Russia's view as to the role of the mistake of fact doctrine in cases involving the shootdown of civil aircraft. Indeed, Russia's position is solely focused on the Montreal Convention, and not the Chicago Convention on International Civil Aviation or customary international law more generally. This argument bears a connection with the functioning of the Montreal Convention. Indeed, this treaty regulates criminal conduct that is, in this case, dependent on intentional action. This all but confirms the rule set out in this chapter: if the primary rule (here Article 1 (1) (*b*) of the Montreal Convention) requires a certain mental element, then the mistake of fact can be accepted as an excuse to the extent that the error in question negates this mental element.[78] Elsewhere, the mistake would not appear to have any relevance. Despite its stubbornness regarding the mistake of fact argument, the Russian Federation itself recognizes this. It cited Trapp's observations on States' reactions to aircraft shootdowns, where it is pointed out that '[w]hen states condemn a use of military force against a civil aircraft or airport, they generally do so within the parameters of the Chicago Convention and customary international law rather than through an invocation of the Montreal Convention.'[79] Thus, 'State practice also shows that the downing of a civilian aircraft in error is not considered a terrorist act falling under the Montreal Convention.'[80]

The parties do not address whether these same cases constitute violations of customary international law or any treaty provision outside the Montreal Convention, and indeed they did not need to. This case concerns a treaty claim under the ICSFT, and the Montreal Convention by extension due to the *renvoi* found in the ICSFT.[81] Thus, the two contending parties were not discussing the status of the mistake of fact defense under *general* international law. Since the jurisdiction to hear the case is grounded on Article 24 (1) of the ICSFT, it is clear that the ICJ could not go beyond the 'dispute ... concerning the interpretation or application of th[e] [ICSFT]' to rule on the legality of the shootdown of MH17 under customary international law or the Chicago Convention. Hence, the extent to which this case illustrates the status of the mistake of fact defense for the general law of State responsibility is limited.

Some observations can be made in this respect. The crux of the dispute between Ukraine and Russia in this context is whether the Montreal Convention crime regulated in Article 1 (1) (*b*) requires the perpetrator to be aware of the civilian status of the aircraft that was attacked. Without delving into that issue too deeply, it is worth noting that this article does not mention the status of the victim aircraft at all. Moreover, in context and in light of its object and purpose, the Montreal Convention needs to be interpreted so as to prevent and punish 'unlawful acts against the safety of civil aviation [that] jeopardize the safety of persons and property, seriously affect the operation of air services, and undermine the confidence of the peoples of the

---

78 See Sects. 3.1 and 3.2.3 of this chapter.

79 Russian Federation (2023), para. 289 (emphasis removed).

80 Ibid. See also, para. 291, where Russia surveys some high-profile cases of aircraft shootdown in error.

81 As the reader is aware, Ukraine's claim is also based on the CERD.

world in the safety of civil aviation'.[82] In light of this purpose, it is reasonable to expect the Montreal Convention to grant the widest possible measure of protection to civilian aircraft, and if awareness of the civilian status were required, this would provide a too accessible escape valve for States to argue that the aircraft was not protected from attack.

This is consistent with Article 3 *bis* (*a*) of the Chicago Convention on International Civil Aviation, which requires the victim of the attack to be 'civil aircraft in flight' but does not impose any requirement of awareness on the part of the perpetrator State. These factors point to the conclusion that knowledge of civilian status is not required, just the civilian status itself. If that is the case, then the mistake of fact as to the status of the aircraft would not exonerate the perpetrator, in line with the ILC's commentary to Article 2 of the Articles on State Responsibility.

Predictably, the ICJ's Judgment in this case, handed down on 31 January 2024, did not address the legal question of mistake of fact.

The final example that will be explored is the joint Application filed by Canada, Sweden, Ukraine and the United Kingdom against Iran in June 2023 in the *Aerial Incident of 8 January 2020* case, claiming that the Respondent violated the Montreal Convention when it shot down Ukraine International Airlines Flight PS752 on 8 January 2020. The strike killed all 176 persons on board, who were nationals of the Applicant States. After it became known that the aircraft had been shot down, Iran stated that this incident occurred 'unintentionally due to human error'.[83] The Iranian President characterized this tragedy as an 'unforgiveable mistake', caused by the misidentification of the Boeing 737-800 as a cruise missile.[84]

The Applicants argued *inter alia* that Iran had failed to 'take all practicable measure to prevent the destruction of Flight PS752',[85] and ask the Court to order that Iran publicly acknowledge its internationally wrongful acts and omissions as alleged; publicly apologise to the Applicants and the families of the victims; provide assurances and guarantees of non-repetition; and prosecute or extradite the alleged offenders.[86]

At the present time, Iran has not pronounced itself in response and the case is still in the initial phases of the written proceedings. Whether Iran will defend its actions on the merits (perhaps even relying on some iteration of the theory of mistake) is unclear. If public statements are anything to go by, it is possible that Iran will claim, like the United States did in the USS *Vincennes* incident, that the shootdown was committed in putative self-defense,[87] since Iran's contention is that it reasonably mistook the approaching civilian airplane for a cruise missile. If this is the case, then the arguments formulated in respect of the United States attitude in the *Aerial*

---

[82] See the preamble of the Montreal Convention, para. 1.

[83] Canada et al. (2023), para. 12.

[84] Ibid., para. 12.

[85] Ibid., para. 41 (a).

[86] Ibid., para. 41 (b).

[87] See Chap. 4.

Incident of 3 July 1988 case are equally valid here: full reliance on (putative) self-defense will confirm Iran's agreement with the position that international law does not consider that a mistake of fact prevents a finding that a 'breach' has occurred in the sense of Article 2 of the Articles on State Responsibility.

The aforementioned cases are just the tip of the iceberg. Lamentably, the cases involving the shootdown of civilian aircraft by mistake are far too numerous. The question that confronts international law here is whether the mistake of fact theory should have any exculpatory effect at all. Understandably, the Applicant States in the different cases will come out defending the position that it should not. The arguments are clear and compelling: the scale of human tragedy caused by the destruction of a civil aircraft, including the death of dozens if not hundreds of innocent passengers, cannot be overlooked. The law as it stands would appear to support this position too. There is no State practice that indicates cases where the mistake of fact would allow a State to avoid a finding that a violation of air law has taken place.[88]

The exception is perhaps the specific case of suppression treaties and related instruments of criminal law, where the allocation of responsibility requires a finding of intent, insofar as the mistake of fact is capable of negating that mental element. At the same time, this is the exception that confirms the rule: indeed, many of the rules that govern responsibility for the shootdown of civil aircraft, treaty and customary law included, do *not* require this element at the State level. The State is always under the obligation to prevent this from happening or investigating and prosecuting those responsible when it does. The clear example is Article 3 *bis* (*a*) of the Chicago Convention on International Civil Aviation (and the corresponding international custom), which compels States not to use weapons against civil aircraft in flight and contains no mental requirement or exceptions, save for a reference to the United Nations Charter that will be interpreted in Chap. 4. It follows that generally States are objectively and strictly liable when it comes to the protection of civil aircraft from unlawful attack. It goes without saying that this conclusion is aligned with the policy objective of ensuring the safety and security of international civil aviation, to which all the air law treaties mentioned in this heading are subservient.

Thus, some conclusions may be drawn from this area of the mistake of fact debate.

First, the law of the air appears to align itself with the position at general international law, in the sense that absent a mental requirement in the primary obligation, a mistake of fact is irrelevant for the question whether a 'breach' has taken place for the purposes of identifying an internationally wrongful act.[89] In that sense, Article 3 *bis* and the State practice preceding and following its adoption all confirm that the only exception to the prohibition on the use of weapons against civil aircraft is self-defense, which rules out the theory of mistake of fact at least at the stage of identifying an internationally wrongful act.

---

[88] As mentioned, the author understands this question to be different from the issue of *preclusion* of responsibility, which will be addressed in Chap. 4.

[89] See Article 2 of the Articles on State Responsibility.

Second, given the strict oversight imposed on aviation security and safety, and the advancements in technology, the slice of cases where a mistake of fact is credible or acceptable is vanishingly narrow.

Third, the shootdown of civil aircraft involves more rules than just the international law of the air, and the effects of fragmentation are painfully evident. Any international lawyer involved in a claim of responsibility in an incident like these needs to be familiar also with the position at human rights law, international humanitarian law and even the law on the use of force. The same action can have a widely different reaction under each of these bodies of international law. Fourth, at least from an interpretative perspective, Article 1 (1) (*b*) of the Montreal Convention does not seem to require the perpetrator's knowledge of the civilian status of an aircraft. A corresponding mistake of fact as to this status therefore would not wipe away the perpetrator's criminal responsibility or the State's duty to prevent, investigate and punish, under the Montreal Convention.

3.2.2 Arbitrary Deprivation of Life

The right to life is the supreme right on which all other human rights depend.[90] It is a right from which human rights treaties admit no derogation.[91] It is also the right to which a lot of the mistake of fact debate has referred. The starting point in this respect is that international law does not prohibit deprivations of life per se. The prevailing position under human rights treaties is that what attracts international responsibility is *arbitrary* deprivation of life. Thus, Article 6 (1) of the International Covenant on Civil and Political Rights (ICCPR) provides that

> Every human being has the inherent right to life. This right shall be protected by law. No one shall be arbitrarily deprived of his life.

Under this provision, States are obligated not only to abstain from themselves depriving persons of their lives arbitrarily, but also to exercise due diligence to ensure that this right is respected by non-attributable third parties.[92] To not be qualified as arbitrary, deprivation of life must be legitimate, necessary and proportionate and not be otherwise prohibited by international law.[93] ICCPR Article 6 (1) does not spell out the situations where deprivation of life is legitimate, but the Human Rights Committee's General Comment no 36 mentions self-defense, defense of others and other instances stemming from a threat to life.[94] To be necessary, the force employed in these circumstances must 'represent a method of last resort after other alternatives

[90] HRC (2019), para. 2.

[91] Article 4 (2) of the ICCPR.

[92] HRC (2019), para. 7.

[93] Ibid., para. 12.

[94] Ibid.

have been exhausted or deemed inadequate'.[95] Moreover, to be proportionate, 'the amount of force applied cannot exceed the amount strictly needed for responding to the threat' and 'must be carefully directed, only against the attacker'.[96] In the case of law enforcement authorities, lethal force is only permitted in extreme circumstances, to protect life from an imminent threat.[97]

Against this background, the possibility of using lethal force by mistake suggests itself. And indeed, one answer to this conundrum was provided by the European Court of Human Rights in the 1995 *McCann and others* v. *United Kingdom* case. In 1988, the authorities of the United Kingdom, Spain and Gibraltar received intelligence that the Provisional Irish Republican Army (IRA) planned to orchestrate a terror attack against Ince's Hall in Gibraltar.[98] An advisory group was assembled to counsel the Police Commissioner on how to deal with this terrorist plot.[99] The United Kingdom's Ministry of Defense would have presence in Gibraltar with the purpose of assisting Gibraltar authorities in the arrest of the IRA active service unit (ASU).[100] An evacuation plan was prepared for 7 and 8 March 1988.[101]

On 4 March 1988, a sighting of the ASU was reported in Málaga, Spain.[102] The next day, a police briefing was held in which the Commissioner explained the rules of engagement, including firearms procedures. Some of the basic assumptions transmitted to the soldiers was that the attack would take place on 8 March 1988 during the ceremonial change of the guard at Ince's Hall.[103] The ASU would consist of three persons: Daniel McCann, Sean Savage and a third person later identified as Mairead Farrell, all of whom should be expected to be armed, dangerous and likely to use their weapons if confronted.[104] Moreover, the attack would be orchestrated by using a car bomb.[105] The possibility that the ASU would use an unarmed car to reserve enough space in the assembly area of Ince's Hall for the car bomb was considered but deemed unlikely.[106] The car bomb was most likely going to be detonated through a radio-controlled improvised explosive device (RCIED), since it would be safer for the terrorists and more controllable.[107] Nonetheless, the possibility of a timer instead of a remove-control device was also expected, according to the recollection of some of those who attended the briefing.[108] The soldiers were made aware of

---

[95] Ibid.

[96] Ibid.

[97] Ibid.

[98] ECtHR (1995), para. 13.

[99] Ibid., para. 14.

[100] Ibid., para. 15.

[101] Ibid., para. 19.

[102] Ibid., para. 21.

[103] Ibid., para. 23 (a).

[104] Ibid., para. 23 (b) and (c).

[105] Ibid., para. 23 (d).

[106] Ibid., para. 23 (e).

[107] Ibid., para. 24.

[108] Ibid., para. 25.

the possibility that, if confronted by security forces, the members of the ASU might decide to detonate the device.[109]

On 6 March 1988, at about 12:30 h, a person parked a car at the surveilled parking area near Ince's Hall, fiddled with something between the seats and then stepped out of the vehicle and walked away. Witnesses identified him as Sean Savage.[110] Though initially not identified, it was reported that Daniel McCann and Mairead Farrell crossed the border into Gibraltar at around 14:30 h.[111] At 14:50 h, it was reported that the three suspects had met up and were looking at the white Renault car parked in the car-park near the assembly area of Ince's Hall.[112] At 15:25 h, the identities of the three suspects were positively confirmed.[113]

After the ASU members abandoned the assembly area, the suspect car was examined externally.[114] The vehicle was then identified as a possible or suspected car bomb, since the aerial of the car was rustier than justified by the apparent age of the car.[115] The soldiers not involved in the examination would later testify that they were convinced that it was a car bomb.[116] Thus, the order was given for the military to intervene and effect arrest.[117] Once the soldiers had been deployed for this purpose and were following the suspects, Savage diverged from the group. Two soldiers followed McCann and Farrell, while Savage was followed by the other two.[118]

The two soldiers following McCann and Farrell confronted the two suspects, and one of them drew his weapon. When McCann made a sudden movement interpreted by the soldier as an attempt to trigger the remote detonator of the car bomb, the soldier opened fire on McCann.[119] Immediately, Farrell made a sudden movement for her handbag. The soldier, believing that she might be reaching for the detonator as well, shot her too.[120] At the same time, the other soldier had also opened fire on the two suspects, in the reverse order, but under the same belief that they presented a threat of detonating the car bomb.[121] After shooting Farrell, the first soldier opened fire on McCann again, firing a total of five shots between the two suspects.[122] The other soldier had fired a total of seven shots.[123]

---

[109] Ibid., paras. 28–31.

[110] Ibid., para. 38.

[111] Ibid., para. 43.

[112] Ibid., para. 45.

[113] Ibid., para. 47.

[114] Ibid., para. 48.

[115] Ibid., paras. 48–50.

[116] Ibid., paras. 50–53.

[117] Ibid., para. 54.

[118] Ibid., para. 58.

[119] Ibid., para. 61.

[120] Ibid.

[121] Ibid., para. 62.

[122] Ibid., para. 61.

[123] Ibid., para. 62.

As for Savage, the soldiers following him attempted arrest. The first soldier drew his pistol and told Savage to stop and put his hands up.[124] When the gunfire was heard behind them (presumably from the exchange between the other two soldiers and McCann and Farrell), and Savage made a sudden movement for his right hip, the soldiers opened fire on him, believing too that he was reaching for a detonator.[125] Three of the four soldiers expressly testified that they indeed had intent to kill, since they thought it was the only way to stop the suspects from detonating the device.[126] After the shooting, however, the bodies of the three suspects were inspected and no evidence of weapons or detonating devices was found.[127] No detonating devices were found on the suspected car bomb either.[128] During the investigation, a completely different car was found to contain an explosive device with timers and four detonators.[129]

The representatives of the estates of the three suspects filed a claim with the European Commission of Human Rights, which in turn alleged a violation of Article 2 of the Convention for the Protection of Human Rights and Fundamental Freedoms (European Convention on Human Rights or ECHR). This provision regulates, in paragraph 1 the right to life, and in paragraph 2 the circumstances in which authorities may deprive a person of her life:

> 2. Deprivation of life shall not be regarded as inflicted in contravention of this Article when it results from the use of force which is no more than absolutely necessary:
>
> (*a*) in defence of any person from unlawful violence;
>
> (*b*) in order to effect a lawful arrest or to prevent the escape of a person lawfully detained;
>
> (*c*) in action lawfully taken for the purpose of quelling a riot or insurrection.

The Grand Chamber of the European Court of Human Rights started by reviewing its jurisprudence on the interpretation of Article 2 of the ECHR, including the understanding that deprivation of life is only permissible when it is 'absolutely necessary' to achieve one of the purposes set out in Article 2 (2).[130] According to the Court, the reference to absolute necessity in Article 2 (2) implies a stricter and more compelling test of necessity than is required under other provisions of the ECHR.[131] The force used must also be strictly proportionate to the purpose pursued.[132]

The Court clarified that in determining whether Article 2 of the ECHR was violated, it is not ruling on the criminal responsibility of the individuals involved.[133]

---

124 Ibid., para. 78.

125 Ibid., paras. 78, 79.

126 Ibid., paras. 63, 82.

127 Ibid., para. 93.

128 Ibid., para. 96.

129 Ibid., para. 99.

130 Ibid., paras. 146–150.

131 Ibid., para. 149.

132 Ibid., para. 150.

133 Ibid., para. 173.

It also found that the allegation of premeditated murder by the arresting soldiers was unsubstantiated.[134] To examine the evidence, the Court decided to divide its analysis into two parts, the first concerning the actions of the soldiers, and the second regarding the responsibility of the United Kingdom.[135]

Regarding the actions of the soldiers, the Court found that the soldiers' belief that killing the suspects was absolutely necessary under Article 2 (2) to prevent them from detonating a bomb and causing serious loss of life was honest.[136] Some of the factors that convinced the Court of this conclusion included the following:

- The soldiers were informed by their superiors that there was a car bomb in the area that could be detonated by any of the three suspects through a radio-control device which they might have concealed in their persons.[137]
- They were also told that the suspects could detonate the bomb if confronted and they were likely to be armed and to resist arrest.[138]
- The shooting of McCann and Farrell, according to the evidence, happened at close range after the suspects had made threatening movements as if they were about to detonate the car bomb.[139] The same was true in respect of Savage.[140]
- The fact that they were unarmed and had no detonators was only discovered subsequently.[141]

Thus, the European Court of Human Rights concluded that

> …[T]he use of force by agents of the State in pursuit of one of the aims delineated in paragraph 2 of Article 2 … of the Convention may be justified under this provision … where *it is based on an honest belief which is perceived, for good reasons, to be valid at the time but which subsequently turns out to be mistaken.* To hold otherwise would be to impose an unrealistic burden on the State and its law-enforcement personnel in the execution of their duty, perhaps to the detriment of their lives and those of others.
>
> It follows that, having regard to the dilemma confronting the authorities in the circumstances of the case, the actions of the soldiers *do not, in themselves, give rise to a violation of this provision* …[142]

However, this is not the end of the matter. The crux of the remaining issues, according to the Court, was

> …whether the anti-terrorist operation as a whole was controlled and organised in a manner which respected the requirements of Article 2 … and whether the information and instructions given to the soldiers which, in effect, rendered inevitable the use of lethal force, took adequately into consideration the right to life of the three suspects.[143]

---

[134] Ibid., paras. 179–184.
[135] Ibid., paras. 192–194.
[136] Ibid., para. 200.
[137] Ibid., para. 195.
[138] Ibid., para. 195.
[139] Ibid., para. 196.
[140] Ibid., para. 197.
[141] Ibid., para. 198.
[142] Ibid., para. 200.
[143] Ibid., para. 201.

Thus, the Court turned to the responsibility of the United Kingdom under Article 2 of the ECHR. The Court highlighted a number of shortcomings in the organization and implementation of the anti-terrorist operation. It noted the United Kingdom's failure to arrest the three suspects as they were identified entering Gibraltar.[144] Mindful of the United Kingdom's concern that the evidence to effect arrest might have been insufficient and that the attempted arrest might have alerted the suspects to the authorities' awareness of the terror plot,[145] the Court considered that the danger to Gibraltar's population outweighed the possible consequences of detaining and trying the suspects with insufficient evidence in the individual circumstances of the case.[146] The decision not to arrest them despite knowing the risk they posed was described by the Court as a 'serious miscalculation'.[147]

But the Court took issue especially with the way information was transmitted to the soldiers in preparation for the operation. It noted that a number of conclusions had been reached by the authorities, including that the terrorists would not use a blocking car; that the bomb's detonation was remotely controlled; that the detonation could be triggered by pressing a button; that the suspects would detonate the bomb if confronted; and that they were likely to use weapons to resist arrest.[148] All of these working hypotheses, based on limited intelligence and inferences, were conveyed to the soldiers as facts, and all of them were later discovered to have been erroneous.[149]

Simultaneously, the authorities did not contemplate the possibility that other assumptions may have been warranted, such as the fact that the terror attack was expected on 8 March 1988 might have suggested that the three suspects were on a reconnaissance mission.[150] Many of the conclusions conveyed to the soldiers were oversimplifications.[151] For example, the conclusion that the car may have been a car bomb after a 'cursory external examination' was transmitted to the soldiers as a 'definite indication that there was such a bomb'.[152] All of these facts, taken together, made the eventual use of lethal force by the arresting soldiers 'unavoidable'.[153] Thus, the Court concluded that the United Kingdom had violated Article 2 of the ECHR.[154]

This particular manifestation of the mistake of fact theory has been applied more successfully in subsequent cases. One example is the *Andronicou and Constantinou* v. *Cyprus* case, which concerned the killing of a young woman by law enforcement authorities during a raid. Lefteris Andronicou had held his fiancée, Elsie Constantinou, hostage at their home. After hostage negotiations failed, the police

---

144 Ibid., para. 203.
145 Ibid., para. 204.
146 Ibid., para. 205.
147 Ibid., para. 205.
148 Ibid., para. 206.
149 Ibid., para. 207.
150 Ibid., para. 208.
151 Ibid., para. 208.
152 Ibid., para. 209.
153 Ibid., para. 210.
154 Ibid., paras. 212–214.

raided the home in order to rescue Elsie. Upon entering the home, however, one of the officers was shot by Andronicou.[155] It was established that a second shot from Andronicou's gun hit Elsie.[156] One of the officers saw the others fall backwards. Believing that they had been injured by Andronicou and unaware whether he was armed, the officer shot at Andronicou several times until he was lying on the floor.[157] Another officer had also fired at Andronicou, who died shortly after.[158] Elsie, who was injured in the shoot-out, was taken to the hospital in deep shock. After being operated on and spending some hours in the intensive care unit, Elsie died of her wounds.[159] The inquiry after the incident concluded that at least two of the bullets fired by the officers struck Elsie, and thus a claim was brought that a violation of Article 2 of the ECHR had ensued.

Reaffirming the strict test to be applied under Article 2 of ECHR, the Court cited the *McCann and others* case to confirm that it 'must, in making its assessment, subject deprivations of life to the most careful scrutiny, particularly where deliberate lethal force is used, taking into consideration not only the actions of the agents of the State who actually administer the force but also all the surrounding circumstances, including such matters as the planning and control of the actions under examination'.[160] In this context, the Court found no fault in the planning and implementation of the operation. Indeed, the authorities never lost sight that the incident did not involve hardened criminals or terrorists, but rather an instance of domestic violence.[161] Moreover, the authorities attempted to resolve the incident through dialogue and persuasion up to the very last moment.[162] The authorities' intervention was also warranted considering that there existed a reasonable fear that Elsie's physical integrity or even life was in danger and 'an attempt had to be made to get into the flat, disarm and arrest [Lefteris Andronicou] and free Elsie Constantinou.'[163] Thus, the Court concluded that the rescue operation, intended to free Elsie Constantinou and arrest Lefteris Andronicou, had complied with the requirement of minimizing the resort to lethal force on the part of the law enforcement authorities.

Turning to the officers' administration of force, the Court noted that Andronicou had attempted to kill the first officer who entered the house, and the force used by the officers was a reaction to this initial violence.[164] Although Andronicou was no longer holding his shotgun when the officers who shot him entered the house, the Court considered that they 'honestly believed in the circumstances that it was necessary to kill him in order to save the life of Elsie Constantinou and their own

155 ECtHR (1997), paras. 76–78.

156 Ibid., para. 77.

157 Ibid., para. 78.

158 Ibid., para. 79.

159 Ibid., para. 86.

160 Ibid., para. 171.

161 Ibid., para. 183.

162 Ibid.

163 Ibid., para. 184.

164 Ibid., para. 191.

lives and to fire at him repeatedly in order to remove any risk that he might reach for a weapon.'[165] Thus, in line with its *McCann and others* precedent, the Court concluded that this honest belief was enough to trigger the appropriate exceptions under Article 2 (2) of the ECHR. Again, not exonerating the soldiers for action taken on the basis of 'an honest belief which is perceived, for good reasons, to be valid at the time but subsequently turns out to be mistaken' would impose too heavy a burden on the law enforcement authorities to the detriment of their own lives and the lives of others.[166] Moreover, the accuracy of the officers' fire was necessarily impaired by the actions of Andronicou in 'clinging on to [Elsie Constantinou]' and thus 'exposing her to risk'.[167] Hence, the use of force by the authorities, though regrettably resulting in the death of Elsie Constantinou, had been 'absolutely necessary' to fulfil at least one objective under Article 2 (2) of the ECHR and therefore in full accordance with the right to life.

These findings are reaffirmed in subsequent jurisprudence, such as the *Bubbins* v. *United Kingdom* and *Huohvanainen* v. *Finland* cases. The case law reveals that European human rights law recognizes a well-defined and fully realized doctrine of mistake of fact applicable to the resort to lethal force by law enforcement. The policy objectives of including this defense are also clear since it provides law enforcement agents with sufficient latitude to implement their duties without impairing the essence of the right to life. As the European Court repeats in each of these cases, to deny officers the benefit of this legal defense would undermine the exercise of their functions and render the implementation of the ECHR less practical and effective. At the same time, the latitude given to law enforcement agents is not absolute, since the specific resort to force must be compared with the background of the operation. Thus, a mistake of fact only operates fully if the Government has taken all reasonable precautions to minimize the risk that resort to lethal force will be necessary. This circumscribes this theory of mistake of fact within acceptable parameters that do not endanger life enough to breach the underlying logic of Article 2 of the ECHR. The State is responsible for a deprivation of life in this paradigm if it failed to organize the specific operation in a way that would respect the right to life of potential victims of the use of force. In such cases, the mistake of fact ceases to operate as a defense and becomes the source of liability, since it turns into proof of the deficient and negligent structure of the operation. Thus, while the individual officers or soldiers might be blameless under international law on account of the mistake of fact, the State is not. Conversely, when the operation is planned carefully and taking full account of the policies underlying Article 2 of the ECHR, the mistake of fact theory exonerates both the agents on the ground, and the State responsible for the operation.

All of this needs to be considered also in light of the jurisprudence of the European Court of Human Rights regarding the deference to be given to fact-finders and the scrutiny of the evidence. The European Court is not a tribunal of first instance and is not in the position to take evidence or fully reassess it. This is especially true in cases

[165] Ibid., para. 192.

[166] Ibid.

[167] Ibid.

involving the use of lethal force, as the Court cannot substitute its own judgment for that of the agent who needed to avert an 'honestly perceived threat'.[168]

A relevant factor is that the European Court's standard for the application of the mistake of fact theory appears to be based on *subjective* perception. The emphasis is on honest and genuine mistakes made by the law enforcement agent, in light of the circumstances of the operation. At the same time, this does not mean that this subjective theory of mistake is without its safeguards. Although objective reasonability is not expected in respect of the agent, the State's duty to plan and implement the operation with full respect for the right to life and the need to minimize the use of force becomes an objective parameter to assess responsibility. Indeed, even if the agent is entirely blameless due to a genuinely held (but ultimately mistaken) belief, the State must continue to ensure that the circumstances in which this may occur are brought to a minimum. This standard does not depend on the State's perception but on the objective structure of the law enforcement operation itself. For example, the European Court faulted the United Kingdom in the *McCann and others* case for failing to detain the three suspects as they entered Gibraltar, imposing an objective standard based on the wisdom of hindsight, as it were, on the value judgment conducted by the authorities at the time. The identification of such 'background failures'[169] and shortcomings in the planning and implementation of the operation thus brings an objective element to the calculus that fully accords with the position at general international law that the State's responsibility is strict and not based on fault. This has led authors like Melzer to conclude that the standard of mistake of fact employed by the European Court of Human Rights requires both subjective genuineness and objective reasonability.[170]

The precedents cited in this section are circumscribed to the European context. The question is whether the same reasoning could be applied at the universal level under Article 6 of the ICCPR. Although some authors have taken the view that the right to life has the same standard in substance under the ICCPR,[171] the Human Rights Committee's General Comment no 36 does not answer this question outright. The reason may be that, while the ECHR has a textual basis for the theory of mistake of fact, the ICCPR does not. Under Article 2 of the ECHR, it is 'intentional' deprivation of life that is prohibited. This stands in contrast to Article 6 ICCPR, which employs the term 'arbitrar[y]' instead. The difference is subtle, but not non-existing. The Human Rights Committee has expressly dispelled the existence of an automatic connection between arbitrariness and intentionality in the context of deprivations of life found to violate Article 6 of the ICCPR. In its General Comment no 36, the Committee clarifies that Article 6 prohibits either intentional deprivations of life (like Article 2 of the ECHR), or unintended but 'otherwise foreseeable and preventable life-terminating harm or injury, caused by an act or omission'.[172] According to the

[168] ECtHR (2007), para. 97.

[169] Milanovic (2020b).

[170] Melzer (2009), p. 118.

[171] See e.g. Melzer (2009), pp. 118–120.

[172] HRC (2019), para. 6.

jurisprudence of the European Court of Human Rights as explained in its guide to Article 2 of the ECHR, 'paragraph 2 does not primarily define instances where it is permitted to kill an individual, but describes the situations where it is permitted to "use force" which may result, as an unintended outcome, in the deprivation of life.'[173] This shows that, unlike under Article 6 of the ICCPR, the assessment of unintentional deprivation of life already has Article 2 (2) as one of its primary starting points, a provision which is concerned with situations in which deprivation of life may be exceptionally permitted. While the author is not suggesting that the ECHR is more lenient in its treatment of the right to life than the Covenant, it does appear that Article 6 of the ICCPR adopts a different approach to the question of the volitional element. Thus, while a death caused by a genuine and honest mistake of fact (negating the *animus necandi*) may be excused under Article 2 of the ECHR, either owing to the 'intentional' language in paragraph 1 or the need to implement human rights safeguards that are practical and effective generally, it is not immediately clear that the same will be true for Article 6 of the ICCPR. The fact that Article 2 (2) of the ECHR lists specifically circumscribed exceptions to the protection of the right to life, and Article 6 ICCPR does not, also confirms that the approaches under Article 2 of the ECHR regarding mistakes of fact are not automatically transposable to the Covenant. This suggests that the answer to the titular question of this chapter, in the context of Article 6 of the ICCPR, will require specific interpretation and review of precedent under this provision.

Article 6 is categorical in that '[n]o one shall be arbitrarily deprived of his life.' As is stated in General Comment no 36, the notion of arbitrariness involves questions of inappropriateness, injustice, lack of predictability and due process of law.[174] The State's affirmative duty to protect life includes punishing both intentional and negligent homicide as well as unnecessary use of firearms.[175] The Human Rights Committee has not yet addressed the question of mistake of fact in response to individual communications or in its General Comments. However, some views adopted by this human rights body under ICCPR Article 6 may shed some light on how to deal with these cases.

The first example that will be used under Article 6 of the ICCPR is *Camargo (on behalf of Suárez de Guerrero)* v. *Colombia*, considered by the Committee on 31 March 1982. The individual communication concerned a raid by law enforcement agents that resulted in the death of seven innocent persons. The judicial authorities of Colombia had ordered the raid to a home where it was believed that Mr. Miguel de German Ribon, former Ambassador of Colombia to France, was being held after being kidnapped some days earlier by a guerrilla organization.[176] When the law enforcement agents entered the home, however, the former Ambassador was not there. The police patrol decided to hide within the home, waiting for the 'suspected

[173] ECtHR (2022), para. 101.

[174] HRC (2019), para. 12.

[175] Ibid., para. 20.

[176] HRC (1982), para. 1.2.

kidnappers' to return.[177] They then killed seven persons, identified by the Human Rights Committee as innocent,[178] as they entered the home, without warning or the opportunity to surrender,[179] and at point-blank range. The Human Rights Committee was then called upon to rule on whether a violation of ICCPR Article 6 had been committed by the Colombian authorities.

It is unclear from the text of the Committee's views whether Colombia made a plea of justifiable error by the law enforcement authorities, in the same sense as it was done in the *McCann and others* case before the European Court of Human Rights. It is also doubtful that any such error could be sustained on the facts. The substratum of the mistake of fact theory, however, is hiding under the surface. Indeed, the operation was ostensibly ordered on the belief that former Ambassador Miguel de German Ribon was being held prisoner in the home and that the victims were the alleged kidnappers. The officers also reported that the victims had been allegedly armed and were shot upon in self-defense. These allegations were all disproven by the evidence. The argument of the claimant, of course, was that there were all mere pretexts to justify law enforcement overreach and abuse of authority, as well as extrajudicial killing:

> The author alleges that seven persons – including María Fanny Suárez de Guerrero – were arbitrarily killed by the police, that the police action was unjustified and that it has been inadequately investigated by the Colombian authorities. ... He further alleges that there have been other cases of arbitrary killings by the army and the police *on the pretext that they were dealing with suspicious people* and that it has later been proved that *the victims were either innocent or persecuted for political reasons.*[180]

In response to this fact pattern, the Human Rights Committee pointed out that, since the right to life under Article 6 of the ICCPR was the supreme right of the human being, deprivations of life by State authorities ought to be considered as 'matters of the utmost gravity'.[181] The Committee had concluded that the killing of the seven victims had been the result of 'deliberate action' by the police patrol and thus 'the deprivation of life was intentional',[182] i.e. at the very least, not accidental or fortuitous. No opportunity was given to the victims to surrender or to give explanations.[183] Moreover, there was no evidence that the killing was a necessary measure of self-defense or defense of others, or to effect the arrest or prevent the escape of the suspects.[184] Crucial for our inquiry is the Committee's consideration that

> ... the victims were *no more than suspects of the kidnapping* which had occurred some days earlier and *their killing by the police deprived them of all the protections of due process of law* laid down by the Covenant. In the case of Mrs. María Fanny Suárez de Guerrero, the

[177] Ibid., para. 1.2.

[178] Ibid., para. 1.2.

[179] Ibid., para. 1.3.

[180] Ibid., para. 1.4 (emphasis added).

[181] Ibid., para. 13.1.

[182] Ibid., para. 13.2.

[183] Ibid.

[184] Ibid.

> forensic report showed that she had been shot several times after she had already died from a heart attack. There can be no reasonable doubt that her death was caused by the police patrol.[185]

Thus, the Committee concluded that Colombia had violated Article 6 of the ICCPR.[186]

Another relevant case is *Burrell* v. *Jamaica*, which was considered by the Human Rights Committee on 18 July 1996. On 31 October 1993, Rickly Burrell was a death row inmate in St. Catherine's District Prison in Jamaica. At the time, some prison warders had been taken hostage by inmates and Burrell was shot 'in cold blood' by the prison authorities in this context.[187] The State had acknowledged that Burrell's killing had been in accident, committed in the confusion caused by the attempt to rescue the hostages. It is worth noting that the warders taken hostage mostly sustained minor injuries, which according to counsel for Burrell pointed to the need to resort to non-lethal force in response.[188] The Committee took notice of these facts and reasoned as follows:

> The Committee has carefully examined all information forwarded by both counsel and the State party in relation to Mr. Burrell's death following the hostage taking of some warders at St. Catherine prison's death row section, on 31 October 1993. ... The Committee notes that counsel has alleged, on the basis of letters received from other inmates in St. Catherine Prison, that Mr. Burrell was shot after the warders were already released, and thus *the need for force no longer existed*. The Committee notes that *the State party itself has acknowledged that Mr. Burrell's death was the unfortunate result of confusion on the side of the warders, who panicked when seeing some of their colleagues being threatened by the inmates*, and that the report submitted by the State party acknowledges that the shooting continued after the warders were rescued.[189]

The Committee therefore concluded that Jamaica had failed to comply with Article 6 (1) of the ICCPR.[190]

These two cases under Article 6 of the ICCPR illustrate a series of points. The concept of 'arbitrariness' that serves as parameter for the legality of the use of force by State authorities is rather wide, which is consistent with the fact that State killings are to be considered of the greatest gravity. The State needs to prove that there was a justifiable reason for the officers to engage in the use of lethal force (i.e., *legitimacy*: usually self-defense, defense of others, or as a necessary measure for effecting arrest or preventing the escape of the suspect), and that the specific use of force was *necessary* (there existed no alternative ways to fulfil the legitimate objective) and *proportionate* (the force used was commensurate with the threat posed by the victim).

The *Camargo* case illustrates that deliberate killing without justification violates Article 6 of the ICCPR. But the *Burrell* case, on the other hand, proves that killings

---

185 Ibid. (emphasis added).

186 Ibid., para. 13.3.

187 HRC (1996), para. 2.13.

188 Ibid., paras. 2.8, 5.4.

189 Ibid., para. 9.5 (emphasis added).

190 Ibid.

found by the Committee to have been *accidental* (non-intentional) were also at variance with the right to life. The underlying policy concern appears to be that killing by State authorities, which is a charge of exceptional gravity, is subject to the strictest safeguards. Error by the State is not an excuse but a failure of due care. Article 6 of the ICCPR clearly does not give law enforcement agents wide discretion in implementing their functions, as they must at all times safeguard the right to life of the persons that may be affected by their operations.

Although debate can be had as to the merit of the justifications given by the States in the cases above, the interesting part is that the Human Rights Committee does not attempt to entertain them in applying Article 6. They do not even enter the calculus as to whether the killing was arbitrary or not. In *Camargo*, a killing based on the 'belief' that a former Ambassador had been held hostage by the victims and that the victims were armed in no way negated the Committee's conclusion that their killing had been 'intentional' and 'deliberate'. Indeed, framing it in a similar sense as the *McCann and others* case, whether the law enforcement agents may have had a 'genuine and honest belief' or not was irrelevant because the agents had deliberately chosen to aim their guns at the victims and pulled the trigger. The killing was not less arbitrary due to this fact. In the *Burrell* case, one can find the same policy concern. The State's error was considered by the Committee, not as a mitigating circumstance, but as the source of liability. Indeed, the Committee's conclusion that the 'circumstances' indicated that the State party had 'failed in taking effective measures to protect Mr. Burrell's life' included the acknowledgement by Jamaica that the killing was 'the unfortunate result of confusion on the side of the warders, who panicked when seeing some of their colleagues being threatened by the inmates' and that it had happened 'after the warders were rescued'. The Committee's handling of this case suggested that the 'confusion' and 'panic' of the prison authorities was not an excuse for the killing of Mr. Burrell, but rather evidence of their lapse in judgment and readiness to use excessive force.

There is a separate policy concern that shines through in the Human Rights Committee's views in the *Camargo* case. Indeed, the Committee does not only fault Colombia for the excess displayed by the officers in their use of lethal force. It also connects the safeguards of the right to life with another guarantee: the overarching right to due process under Articles 14 and 15 of the ICCPR. The connecting tissue found by the Committee was the strict guidelines for the death penalty found in Article 6 itself:

> The right enshrined in this article [Article 6] is the supreme right of the human being. It follows that the deprivation of life by the authorities of the State is a matter of the utmost gravity. *This follows from the article as a whole and in particular is the reason why paragraph 2 of the article lays down that the death penalty may be imposed only for the most serious crimes.*[191]

Then, as cited previously, when finding a violation of Article 6 in the *Camargo* case the Committee placed great focus on the fact that the victims were 'no more than suspects of the kidnapping which had occurred some days earlier' and that 'their

---

[191] HRC (1982), para. 13.1 (emphasis added).

killing by the police deprived them of all the protections of due process of law laid down by the Covenant'.[192] This is a critical point. The killing of the seven victims, grounded on a mistake of fact or not, was incompatible with Article 6 because the belief that they were the perpetrators of the kidnapping (i.e. their status as suspects) signified that they were entitled to a due process of law following the safeguards imposed by the ICCPR. Their killing, even if presumably by mistake or accident, prevented them from appearing before a court of law to vindicate their substantive and procedural rights. Accepting that law enforcement could kill an innocent person based on a mistake of fact could entail an implicit authorization to kill without due process of law. It would shift the burden of proof from the State and its law enforcement authorities onto the victim of the killing. This supports the inference that a transposition of the theory of mistake of fact onto the universal system for the protection of human rights is not compatible with Article 6 of the ICCPR.

Now, this does not mean that the European Court's approach is fully disconnected from the Human Rights Committee's approach to ICCPR Article 6. Indeed, General Comment no 36 does indicate that ICCPR Article 6, like Article 2 of the ECHR, requires the State to carefully plan and implement its law enforcement operations 'in a manner consistent with the need to minimize the risk they pose to human life'.[193] The case cited by the Committee in support for this position is, indeed, *McCann and others*.[194] The difference is that the interpretation of Article 6 of the ICCPR is focused on the responsibility of the State, and not the blameworthiness of the actions taken by the State's agent in the heat of the moment. This is key. It means that while the European Court of Human Rights distinguishes between the State's actions (the planning of the operation, where mistakes are incriminatory) and the actions of the agent (the actual administration of the force, where mistakes are exculpatory), the Human Rights Committee focuses only on the responsibility of the State as an objective whole. By taking the individual blameworthiness out of the equation, the ICCPR's interpretation leaves no gap for the mistake of fact theory. General Comment no 36 shows that a distinction is made along a different axis, between State responsibility for arbitrary deprivation of life on one hand, and individual criminal or civil responsibility for homicide, wrongful death or similar delicts on the other. Not all killings that run afoul of Article 6 of the ICCPR should translate automatically to individual crimes under national law. As explained by Mavronicola in her submission to the Human Rights Committee in preparation for General Comment no 36, these two concepts are not coterminous in international law and should be kept that way, as it would prevent individuals from being criminally punished for systemic errors while allowing the State to refine its operation in accordance with the right to life.[195]

The same idea is echoed in a different context by Lahmann.[196] Indeed, to draw a different distinction or impose a subjective standard on the *State*'s responsibility,

[192] Ibid., para. 13.2.

[193] HRC (2019), para. 12.

[194] See HRC (1982), footnote 32.

[195] Mavronicola (2017), paras. 10, 17, 18.3.

[196] Lahmann (2020).

including by importing a mistake of fact doctrine (sometimes referred to as the 'honest belief test'[197]) could dilute the right to life.[198] As described by Martin when commenting on the *Bubbins* v. *United Kingdom* case, the standard of mistake of fact used by the European Court of Human Rights runs the risk of reversing the onus of proving the legitimacy of the use of lethal force. 'Given that there were a number of noticeable errors and questionable decisions made in the conduct of the operation, it would seem that the Court will require an extremely high level of error, ineptitude or bad judgement before it will find a breach of' the right to life.[199] These considerations lead the author to conclude that the universal human rights system does not accept the mistake of fact doctrine as a justification for otherwise arbitrary deprivation of life.

This conclusion is confirmed by referring to customary international law under Article 31 (3) (*c*) of the Vienna Convention on the Law of Treaties. Indeed, there are numerous cases involving use of force by State agents, based on mistakes of fact, that have been ruled as internationally wrongful. A good example is the *Kling* case, which Iran used as precedent in the ICJ's *Aerial Incident of 3 July 1988* case to show that the United States had violated international law by shooting down Iran Air Flight 655 even if by mistake.[200]

The case concerned the wrongful killing of August Francis Kling by the authorities of Mexico. Kling was employed by the Texas Company of Mexico, S. A. On 23 January 1921, Kling and other company employees returned from Zacamixtle to the company's camp and stood leisurely near the company property. Some of Kling's companions, 'in fun',[201] started to fire their revolvers into the air. Unbeknownst to them, the Mexican authorities had been following them and, once the group had started firing into the air, the authorities opened fire upon them, striking Kling, who died of his injuries two months later. Among the arguments raised by Mexico in its defense, it alleged that the soldiers had acted 'within their duty in repelling an aggression which, *real or imaginary, had all the aspects of an attack* by a party which, because of the hour and their behavior, might be considered as marauder.'[202] On 1930, the General Claims Commission (Mexico and United States) rejected this argument ruling that

> In cases of this kind it is mistaken action, error in judgment, or reckless conduct of soldiers for which a government in a given case has been held responsible. The international precedents reveal the application of principles as to the very strict accountability for mistaken action.[203]

In support of this position, the Commission relied in its previous cases, particularly the *Falcón* incident, a case where United States soldiers, presumably in self-defense,

[197] Ibid., paras. 14–16; cf. Melzer (2009), pp. 106–113, 118.

[198] Mavronicola (2017), para. 17.

[199] Martin (2006), p. 246.

[200] See Sect. 3.2.1 of this chapter.

[201] General Claims Commission (1930), p. 576.

[202] Ibid., p. 578 (emphasis added).

[203] Ibid., p. 579.

shot upon men believed to have been engaged in smuggling, who failed to obey orders to halt; and the *García and Garza* case, where a United States lieutenant fired upon a raft propelled in violation of United States laws, without intent to hit the tripulants but rather with the purpose of scaring them 'to cause them to return to the American side in order that he might arrest them'.[204] In the last case, the Commission noted that a violation of international law was found even though the evidence did not indicate malice or intention to kill, since this 'error of judgment' justified an award against the United States.[205] The Commission pointed out that the Kling shooting was not 'the result of any attempt to secure the apprehension of a person endeavoring to escape arrest'.[206] Thus,

> *Whatever excuse might be made for the action of the Mexican soldiers*, their conduct must be considered to have been *indiscreet, unnecessary and unwarranted*. There are also numerous international incidents of this kind, cases not concerned with attempted arrests, in which damages have been assessed for mistaken, unnecessary, indiscreet or reckless action.[207]

The Commission then proceeded to cite other cases where reparation was granted despite the presence of mistakes of fact, such as the *Dogger Bank* case in 1904, where an award was made against Russia for shooting a British ship despite the fact that Russia had apparently believed to be responding to approaching (hostile) Japanese torpedoes; a case where Germany paid compensation for the shooting of a French person, which was the result of a soldier's misunderstanding of his orders; and the case of *The Jessie, Thomas F. Bayard and Pescawha*, in which '[t]he general rule as to the responsibility of a government for errors in judgment of its representatives' was reiterated to show that, even though the United States naval authorities had acted in good faith, this could only be 'invoked by the officers in explanation of their conduct to their own Government', but its effect was merely to show that 'their conduct constituted an error in judgment', for which 'any government is responsible to other governments'.[208]

These cases are consistent with the interpretation given by the Human Rights Committee to Article 6 of the ICCPR. Indeed, they indicate that mistakes of fact committed by State authorities in the administration of lethal force are the source of responsibility rather than a justification.[209] Used as interpretative guidance under Article 31 (3) (*c*) of the Vienna Convention on the Law of Treaties, they confirm that the theory of mistake of fact developed by the European Court of Human Rights might not be applicable outside the regime established by the ECHR.

---

[204] Ibid.

[205] Ibid., p. 580.

[206] Ibid.

[207] Ibid. (emphasis added).

[208] See Ibid., pp. 580–581.

[209] The question whether a mistake of fact may affect the analysis of preclusion of wrongfulness, including the question of distress, will be addressed in Chap. 4.

3.2.3 *Mistake of Fact in International Criminal Law and Related Fields*

Unlike other areas of international law, the theory of mistake of fact is expressly recognized in Article 32 of the Rome Statute of the International Criminal Court. Article 32 (1) reads as follows:

> A mistake of fact shall be a ground for excluding criminal responsibility only if it negates the mental element required by the crime.

This provision can be described as somewhat redundant. Indeed, as Schabas explains, '[a]n offender who lacks knowledge of an essential fact does not possess the guilty mind or *mens rea* necessary for conviction.'[210] This is a direct result of the fact that the primary norm in all these international criminal law provisions requires a particular mental state, be it a general intent or an additional *dolus specialis*. The ILC itself recognizes the application of a subjective approach when it comes to the specific intent of genocide.[211]

The impact of a mistake of fact for the establishment of individual criminal responsibility under international law is evidenced too by the International Criminal Court's Elements of Crimes. Particularly, the elements of Article 6 (e), which regulates genocide by forcibly transferring children, includes a requirement of knowledge: 'The perpetrator knew, or should have known, that the [victims] were under the age of 18 years.'[212] A similar mental requirement is found in the elements to the crimes under Articles 8 (2) (*b*) (*xxvi*) and 8 (2) (*e*) (*vii*), which regulate the war crime of conscription and enlistment of children under the age of fifteen into armed forces or for active participation in hostilities in international and non-international armed conflicts respectively. The Elements of Crime require that 'The perpetrator knew or should have known that such person or persons were under the age of 15 years.'[213] In that sense, a mistake of fact affecting the age of the victim would negate the mental element required for genocide or the war crime of conscripting, enlisting or using children in armed conflict. But as Schabas explains, the language 'knew or should have known' in both provisions suggests that the perpetrator's lack of awareness of this age cannot be the result of negligence as otherwise the mistake of fact defense will be unavailable.[214] In any case, if the defense is not accepted, a mistake of fact may be considered by the Court as a mitigating circumstance at the sentencing stage.[215]

The application of Article 32 (1) of the Rome Statute reveals a degree of fragmentation. Perhaps the best example is the shootdown of MH17, discussed previously in

---

[210] Schabas (2016), 657.

[211] ILC (2001), Art. 2, para. 3.

[212] Elements of Crimes, p. 4, para. 6.

[213] Ibid., pp. 31, 39.

[214] Schabas (2016), 658.

[215] Triffterer and Ohlin (2022), para. 27.

the section regarding air law.[216] It has been argued[217] that this attack could, in principle, fall within the definition of a war crime under Article 8 of the Rome Statute, either for intentionally directing an attack against civilians or civilian objects,[218] or launching an attack knowing that it will cause incidental loss of life or injury to civilians or damage to civilian objects that is disproportionate in relation to the anticipated military advantage.[219] The issue that has been pointed out is that, if the argument is accepted that the DPR separatists had been laboring under a mistake of fact when shooting down the aircraft (e.g., they were unaware of its civilian status), then individual criminal responsibility for a war crime would be negated under Article 32 (1) of the Rome Statute.[220] At the same time, this provision would not prevent a finding that the shootdown violated the right to life of the victims under universal human rights law.[221] It also would not be dispositive for the question whether the DPR separatists are liable under Article 1 (1) (*b*) of the Montreal Convention or whether the Russian Federation violated the ICSFT.

It is in this light that the biggest problem of Article 32 (1) arises. It is clear that this article would negate the criminal responsibility of *individuals* for international crimes within the jurisdiction of the International Criminal Court. But would it also negate the responsibility of the *State* under general international law for the breach of corresponding *jus cogens* obligations? This question is not easy to answer. For one, it is unquestionable that Article 32 (1) does not codify *jus cogens*, but this does not settle the issue. The author believes that the ILC's position regarding the role of subjective elements in State responsibility[222] also applies here. If the definition of the crime in question requires a mental element, there is no reason that a mistake of fact that negates it should not be able to prevent the establishment of an internationally wrongful act. Indeed, the definition of genocide is the key example offered by the ILC in its commentary on the issue.[223] Consider a mistake of fact that negates the knowledge of State authorities regarding the civilian status of an object before an attack.

It should be clarified that this does not mean that the theory of mistake of fact has somehow been elevated to a peremptory norm. Rather, it prevents an essential precondition of the *jus cogens* norm from being fulfilled. At the same time, the obligations of States under *jus cogens* are far more extensive than only abstaining from committing international crimes. A good example is the prohibition of genocide. Article I of the Genocide Convention reads that the obligation of States is to 'prevent' and 'punish' this crime. The duty not to engage in genocidal acts comes by

[216] See Sect. 3.2.1 of this chapter.

[217] E.g., Heller (2014).

[218] See Article 8 (2) (*b*) (*i*), (*b*) (*ii*), (*e*) (*i*) and (*e*) (*i*) of the Rome Statute.

[219] See Article 8 (2) (*b*) (*iv*) of the Rome Statute.

[220] Heller (2014).

[221] See Sect. 3.2.2 of this chapter.

[222] See Sect. 3.1 of this chapter.

[223] ILC (2001), Art. 2, para. 3.

implication.[224] The duty of prevention and punishment has been recognized by the ICJ as an obligation of conduct,[225] where the fact that the State committed an objectively reasonable mistake of fact may be a relevant factor in determining whether its international responsibility has been engaged.

To avoid too large a loophole for international criminal responsibility, the author believes that the approach to be followed in applying Article 32 (1) of the Rome Statute to the State should mirror the European Court of Human Rights' approach to mistakes of fact in respect of arbitrary deprivation of life[226] and the question of responsibility by catalysis.[227] If the international crime is committed by a State organ under the influence of a mistake of fact, the State should not be exonerated unless it can be established that it adopted the necessary measures internally to minimize the risk of such an international crime occurring and that it has taken action to prevent or punish it. Such a position would make the theory of mistake of fact come full circle, since it would take account of the subjective elements of the crime without forgetting the objective nature of the State's responsibility under international law. It would also be consistent with the different modes of criminal liability recognized in the Rome Statute, especially the criminal responsibility of civilian and military superiors for the actions of their subordinates according to Article 28. In such a case, the State that fails to fulfil this standard would be liable for committing the crime itself, since the acts of its organ are fully attributable to it (both legally and in fact) regardless of the actor's subjective perceptions.[228] The lack of proper safeguards in the State's law and procedure could be taken as actual evidence of criminal intent negating a plea of mistake at the State level. Of course, if criminal intent can be established at the State level, then this would be enough, *a fortiori*, to trigger the State's responsibility for the attributable conduct. The same reasoning extends to situations where it is a non-State actor that engages in international criminal behavior. The State has the obligation of conduct to ensure that its territory is not utilized by third parties to breach international law. If the individual that committed the crime under the influence of a mistake of fact is not a State actor, the State will only be off the hook for its own failure of due diligence if it can prove that it undertook all actions available to it to prevent the crime, minimize the risk of occurrence and punish the perpetrator. If it fails to do so, the position of the author is that the State would not be responsible for the underlying crime itself, since no ground of attribution can be established. Rather, the State would be responsible for its own failure of monitoring, preventing, controlling and punishing the violation.

In a related way, the theory of mistake of fact has significant importance in the field of international humanitarian law. Here the State's duty of due diligence applies as well. As the ICJ stated in *Wall*, it follows from common Article 1 that 'every State Party to [the Geneva Conventions], whether or not it is a party to a specific conflict,

---

[224] ICJ (2007), paras. 155–165.

[225] Ibid., para. 430.

[226] See Sect. 3.2.2 of this chapter.

[227] See Sect. 3.2.4 of this chapter.

[228] ICJ (2007), paras. 155–165.

is under an obligation to ensure that the requirements of the instruments in question are complied with'.[229] According to the International Committee for the Red Cross' analysis of the I Geneva Convention, common Article 1 contains an 'obligation of means, whose content depends on the specific circumstances, in particular the *foreseeability of the violations and the State's knowledge thereof*, the gravity of the breach, the means reasonably available to the State and the degree of influence it exercises over the private persons'.[230]

Another ambit of great relevance is duty of States not to direct attacks against civilians and civilian objects under international humanitarian law. In this respect, Article 57 (2) (*a*) (*i*) of Additional Protocol I provides as follows:

> With respect to attacks, the following precautions shall be taken:
>
> (*a*) those who plan or decide upon an attack shall:
>
> (*i*) do everything feasible to verify that the objectives to be attacked are neither civilians nor civilian objects and are not subject to special protection but are military objectives within the meaning of paragraph 2 of Article 52 and that it is not prohibited by the provisions of this Protocol to attack them…

The rest of Article 57 provides further limitations to this principle. Under paragraph 2 (*a*) (*ii*), the State must also take precautions in the choice of means and methods of war to avoid or minimize the incidental risk to civilian life and objects. Paragraph 2 (*a*) (*iii*) imposes the duty to refrain from launching the attack if it would cause incidental loss of civilian life, injury to civilians or damage to civilian objects, which would not be militarily necessary. Finally, paragraph 2 (*b*) states that the attack must be discontinued or cancelled it 'it becomes apparent that the objective is not a military one or is subject to special protection' or that the attack may be expected to cause disproportionate incidental death, injury, or destruction.

According to Milanovic, this provision and others related to it establish a regime allowing for objectively reasonable mistakes of fact.[231] Thus, if a State implements all feasible precautions in accordance with international law to verify that the target of its military operation does not include civilians or civilian objects, it would appear that the mistaken death of a civilian, however unfortunate, would not automatically breach international humanitarian law.[232] Melzer posits that the determination of whether the targeted killing of a particular individual is militarily necessary must be done in good faith; thus, there is some tolerance for errors where the assessment was done within the limits of honest judgment in accordance with contemporaneous facts.[233]

A special case is presented by the crime of aggression regulated in Article 8 *bis* of the Rome Statute. Under this provision, the crime of aggression is defined as the

---

[229] ICJ (2004), para. 158.

[230] ICRC (2016), para. 150 (emphasis added).

[231] Milanovic (2020a).

[232] Ibid.

[233] Melzer (2009), p. 408.

'planning, preparation, initiation or execution, by a person in a position effectively to exercise control over or to direct the political or military action of a State, of an act of aggression which, by its character, gravity and scale, constitutes a manifest violation of the Charter of the United Nations.' Scholars have considered under which circumstances a mistake of fact could negate the criminal responsibility of an individual perpetrator under this provision. Triffterer and Ohlin explain that, under the Elements of Crimes, there is no requirement that the perpetrator made a legal evaluation of the 'manifest' character of the violation of the United Nations Charter; rather, all that is required is that the perpetrator was aware of the factual circumstances that established that the use of force by the State under her control or direction was inconsistent with the Charter.[234] Thus, these authors argue that if, for instance, a national leader were to command the armed forces to orchestrate an attack on the genuine but ultimately mistaken belief that her State was to be attacked by another country, invoking self-defense under Article 51 of the United Nations Charter, then the mistake of fact defense would operate on the basis of Article 32 (1) of the Rome Statute and the leader would be exonerated of international criminal responsibility.[235]

However, the narrow scope of this defense is to be acknowledged. Indeed, the authors' analysis is focused on the criminal responsibility of an *individual* under the jurisdiction of the International Criminal Court for the crime of aggression, and not necessarily the responsibility of the *State* that has apparently violated Article 2 (4) of the Charter and the general international law prohibition on the use of force. This is acknowledged by the authors themselves, by pointing out that the crime of aggression is both an individual and a State conduct; it is this second element that must be analyzed under the requirements that public international law imposes on the interstate use of force.[236]

Put in simpler terms, the mere fact that the national leader in the example in question is not internationally responsible for a crime of aggression under Article 8 *bis* of the Statute of the International Criminal Court, does not automatically mean that the State she leads is also exonerated from the violation of Article 2 (4) of the United Nations Charter. These are separate questions dealing with the responsibility of two distinct juridical entities (the national leader and her State, respectively) under different legal frameworks (international criminal law and *jus ad bellum*). Whether this situation of 'putative' self-defense is admissible in public international law will be addressed in Chap. 4.

3.2.4 Responsibility by Catalysis

This final section relates to *responsibility by catalysis*, i.e. the responsibility of the State for the conduct of non-attributable private parties. The State has an obligation

---

[234] Triffterer and Ohlin (2022), paras. 57, 58.

[235] Ibid., para. 59.

[236] Ibid., para. 56.

of vigilance, prevention and control to ensure that these third parties do not injure the rights of other States.[237] This is an obligation of conduct rather than one of results.[238] A failure by the State to exercise due diligence in this respect would translate to a violation of the State's own obligations, as this is not a ground of attribution for the conduct of the private entities.[239]

The landmark case in respect of this strand of responsibility is *Corfu Channel*. In that case, the ICJ ruled that Albania's responsibility for the mining of British warships stemmed from its actual or normative knowledge that the minefield had been laid in its territorial waters, coupled with its failure to exercise the diligence required in the circumstances ('the laying of the minefield … could not have been accomplished without the knowledge of the Albanian Government').[240] The obligations of Albania consisted in 'notifying, for the benefit of shipping in general, the existence of a minefield in Albanian territorial waters' and 'in warning the approaching British warships of the imminent danger to which the minefield exposed them'.[241]

This suggests that an objectively reasonable mistake of fact could excuse the State in the circumstances, if the record shows that the State displayed its best efforts to perform its obligation regardless. In other words, the mistake must undermine the State's endeavors to exercise due diligence. Conversely, the State would breach international law if it could have avoided or overcome the mistake in the specific case by displaying its best efforts. By necessity, the mistake of fact must be objectively excusable in these cases. The author believes that to flesh out this standard (analogical) reference can be had to Article 23 of the ILC's Articles on State Responsibility, construed in this book to cover cases where the mistake of fact results in the material impossibility to perform the obligation.[242] To be clear, in this case the mistake of fact would not manifest itself as a circumstance precluding wrongfulness as it would under Article 23 proper. Given that the State's obligation is of conduct and requires due diligence at the primary rule level, the objectively excusable mistake would undermine the 'breach' element directly rather than preclude its wrongfulness.

References

Augustin JV (1998) ICAO and the use of force against civil aerial intruders. Institute of Air and Space Law, McGill University

Heller KJ (2014) MH17 should be framed as murder, not as a war crime. http://opiniojuris.org/2014/08/11/mh-17-framed-murder-war-crime/. Accessed 21 Aug 2023

---

[237] Koskenniemi (2010), p. 50, ILC (1976), pp. 3, 120.

[238] Koskenniemi (2010), p. 50.

[239] ILC (2001), Commentary to Chapter II, para. 3.

[240] ICJ (1949), pp. 18–22.

[241] Ibid., p. 22.

[242] See Chap. 4.

ICRC (2016) Convention (I) for the Amelioration of the condition of the wounded and sick in armed forces in the field (Geneva, 12 Aug 1949). Commentary of 2016. https://ihl-databases.icrc.org/en/ihl-treaties/gci-1949/article-1/commentary/2016. Accessed 21 Aug 2023

Koskenniemi M (2010) Chapter 5. Doctrines of state responsibility. In: Crawford J, Pellet A, Olleson S, Parlett K (eds) The law of international responsibility. Oxford University Press, pp 45–51

Lahmann H (2020) Mistake of fact in putative self-defence against cyber attacks. https://www.ejiltalk.org/mistake-of-fact-in-putative-self-defence-against-cyber-attacks/. Accessed 21 Aug 2023

Lauterpacht H (1927) Private law sources and analogies of international law. Longmans, Greens and Co.

Martin N (2006) Bubbins *v.* United Kingdom: civil remedies and the right to life. Modern L Rev 69:2

Mavronicola N (2017) Submission to the Human Rights Committee on its draft general comment on article 6 of the international covenant on civil and political rights—right to life. Accessed 16 Aug 2023

Melzer N (2009) Targeted killing in international law. Oxford University Press

Milanovic M (2020a) Mistakes of fact when using lethal force in international law: part I. https://www.ejiltalk.org/mistakes-of-fact-when-using-lethal-force-in-international-law-part-i/. Accessed 16 Aug 2023

Milanovic M (2020b) Mistakes of fact when using lethal force in international law: part III. https://www.ejiltalk.org/mistakes-of-fact-when-using-lethal-force-in-international-law-part-iii/. Accessed 16 Aug 2023

Pellet A (2010) Chapter 1. The definition of responsibility in international law. In: Crawford J, Pellet A, Olleson S, Parlett K (eds) The law of international responsibility. Oxford University Press, pp 3–16

Rajaee F (1993) The Iran-Iraq ear: the politics of aggression. University Press of Florida

Schabas W (2016) The international criminal court: a commentary on the Rome statute, 2nd edn. Oxford University Press

Shaw M (2017) International law, 8th edn. Cambridge University Press

Triffterer O, Ohlin C (2022) Article 32. Mistake of fact or mistake of law, 4th edn. In: Ambos (ed) Rome statute of the international criminal court: article-by-article commentary. Beck-Nomos-Hart, pp 1162–1182

Case Law and Related Documents

Canada et al. (2023) Joint application instituting proceedings. In: ICJ, aerial incident of 8 January 2020 (Canada, Sweden, Ukraine and United Kingdom *v.* Islamic Republic of Iran)

ECtHR (1995) Case of McCann and others *v.* United Kingdom (27 Sept 1995). App no 18984/91

ECtHR (1997) Case of Andronicou and Constantinou *v.* Cyprus (9 Oct 1997). 86/1996/705/897

ECtHR (2007) Case of Huohvanainen *v.* Finland. Judgment (13 Mar 2007). App no 57389/00

ECtHR (2022) Guide on Article 2 of the European convention on human rights, updated on 31 Aug 2022

General Claims Commission (Mexico and United States of America) (1930) Lillie S Kling (United States of America) *v.* United Mexican States. Decision (8 Oct 1930). RIAA IV:575–586

HRC (1982) Pedro Pablo Camargo (on behalf of the husband of María Fanny Suárez de Guerrero) *v.* Colombia. Views adopted on 31 Mar 1982. Communication no 45/1979

HRC (1996) Rickly Burrell *v.* Jamaica. Views adopted on 18 Jul 1996. Communication no 546/1993

HRC (2019) General Comment no 36. CCPR/C/GC/36

ICJ (1949) Corfu channel case (United Kingdom/Albania). Judgment. ICJ Rep 1949:4

ICJ (1959) Case concerning the aerial incident of July 27th, 1955 (Israel *v.* Bulgaria). Judgment. ICJ Rep 1959:127
ICJ (1986) Case concerning military and paramilitary activities in and against Nicaragua (Nicaragua *v.* United States of America). Judgment. ICJ Rep 1986:14
ICJ (2004) Legal consequences of the construction of a wall in the occupied Palestinian territory. Advisory opinion. ICJ Rep 2004:136
ICJ (2007) Case concerning application of the convention on the prevention and punishment of the crime of genocide (Bosnia and Herzegovina *v.* Serbia and Montenegro). Judgment. ICJ Rep 2007:43
Iran (1990) Memorial of the Islamic Republic of Iran. In: ICJ, aerial incident of 3 July 1988 (Islamic Republic of Iran *v.* United States of America)
Israel (1958) Memorial of the Government of Israel. In: ICJ, aerial incident of 27 July 1955 (Israel *v.* Bulgaria)
Russian Federation (2021) Counter-memorial of the Russian federation on the case concerning the application of the international convention for the suppression of the financing of terrorism. In: ICJ, application of the international convention for the suppression of the financing of terrorism and of the international convention on the elimination of all forms of racial discrimination (Ukraine *v.* Russian Federation)
Russian Federation (2023) Rejoinder of the Russian Federation. In: ICJ, application of the international convention for the suppression of the financing of terrorism and of the international convention on the elimination of all forms of racial discrimination (Ukraine *v.* Russian Federation)
Ukraine (2018) Memorial of Ukraine. In: ICJ, application of the international convention for the suppression of the financing of terrorism and of the international convention on the elimination of all forms of racial discrimination (Ukraine *v.* Russian Federation)
Ukraine (2022) Reply of Ukraine. In: ICJ, application of the international convention for the suppression of the financing of terrorism and of the international convention on the elimination of all forms of racial discrimination (Ukraine *v.* Russian Federation)
United Kingdom (1958) Memorial submitted by the Government of the United Kingdom of Great Britain and Northern Ireland. In: ICJ, aerial incident of 27 July 1955 (United Kingdom *v.* Bulgaria)
United States (1958) Memorial submitted by the Government of the United States of America. In: ICJ, aerial incident of 27 July 1955 (United States of America *v.* Bulgaria)

International Civil Aviation Organization (ICAO) Documents

Assembly. 19th session. Resolution A19-1. ICAO Doc 9124
Assembly. 24th session. Resolution A24-5. ICAO Doc 9414
Assembly. Resolutions and minutes, 19th session, resolution A19-1. ICAO Doc 9097-C/1016
Council Working Paper. Legal aspects of the safety of civil aircraft flying in the vicinity of, or inadvertently crossing, international frontiers (presented by the secretary general)—Corrigendum no 2. Doc C-WP/2609
Council Working Paper. Safety of commercial aircraft flying in the vicinity of, or inadvertently crossing, international frontiers (presented by the secretary general). Doc C-WP/2153
Council Working Paper. Signals to be used in respect of airspace restrictions—the desirability of devising standard signals for the exchange of messages when an aircraft has committed an infringement of restricted airspace (548th report to the council by the Chairman of the Air Navigation Commission). Doc C-WP/2376
Council. 111th session. ICAO Doc 9441-C/1081
Council. 33rd session. ICAO Doc 7985-C/908
Council. Extraordinary session (Montreal, 15 and 16 Sept 1983) minutes. ICAO Doc 9416-C/1077

United Nations Documents

General Assembly. 10th session. Resolution 927 (X) adopted 14 Dec 1955: question of the safety of commercial aircraft flying in the vicinity of, or inadvertently crossing, international frontiers. A/RES/927(X)

ILC (1976) ILC Yearbook 1976, vol II

ILC (2001) Draft articles on the responsibility of states for internationally wrongful acts, with commentaries thereto. ILC Yearbook 2001, vol II Part Two

Legal Instruments

Articles on the responsibility of states for internationally wrongful acts. ILC Yearbook 2001, vol II Part Two [articles on state responsibility]

Elements of Crimes. Official Records of the Assembly of States Parties to the Rome Statute of the International Criminal Court, first session, New York, 3–10 Sept 2002 (United Nations publication, sales no. E.03.V.2 and corrigendum), part II.B. [Elements of Crimes]

Rome Statute of the International Criminal Court. 17 July 1998. UNTS 2187:3

United Nations Charter. 26 June 1945. UNTS I:1

Vienna Convention on the Law of Treaties. 25 May 1969. UNTS 1155:331

Chapter 4
Mistake of Fact in the Preclusion of Wrongfulness

4.1 Introduction

International law gives States a safety valve to escape from responsibility through the concept of 'circumstances precluding wrongfulness' (CPWs), in specifically defined and exceptional circumstances. In the ILC's codification, CPWs are described as circumstances that justify an 'otherwise well-founded claim for the breach of an international obligation.'[1] Instead of preventing the breach of the obligation, these grounds presuppose that the wrongful act has occurred and instead eliminate the illegal element. Thus, the effect of successfully invoking a CPW is insulating the wrongdoing State from responsibility, so that the underlying conduct will no longer be at variance with international law.

The ILC's Articles on State Responsibility codify six CPWs: consent, self-defense, force majeure, necessity, distress, and countermeasures. Ostensibly missing from this list is the theory of mistake of fact. The question that arises is whether a mistake of fact may produce this effect according to customary international law and, if so, under which conditions. This is altogether a different question than the one addressed in previous chapters since it presupposes that the act or omission was otherwise contrary to an international obligation in force for the State. At the same time, since this question arises at the level of the secondary rule, it no longer directly concerns the content of the primary rule at issue, as was the case when analyzing whether a 'breach' had occurred.[2] Instead, CPWs leave primary rules unaffected, although they limit their effects while the circumstance is in full swing. For instance, in the *Gabčíkovo-Nagymaros Project* case, the ICJ pointed out that

> ... even if a state of necessity is found to exist, it is not a ground for the termination of a treaty. It may only be invoked to exonerate from its responsibility a State which has failed to implement a treaty. Even if found justified, it does not terminate a Treaty; the Treaty may be ineffective as long as the condition of necessity continues to exist; it may in fact be dormant,

[1] ILC (2001), Commentary to Chapter V of Part One, para. 1.

[2] See Chap. 3.

J. P. Hernández Páez, *Mistake of Fact in Public International Law*,
SpringerBriefs in Law, https://doi.org/10.1007/978-3-031-59508-0_4

> but – unless the parties by mutual agreement terminate the Treaty – it continues to exist. As soon as the state of necessity ceases to exist, the duty to comply with treaty obligations revives.[3]

The distinction drawn here between the primary and secondary rule also corresponds roughly to the difference between the law of State responsibility and the law of sources. While the law of the relevant source (e.g. treaty law) determines the existence of the underlying obligation, the law of State responsibility determines the effects attributed to its breach.[4] CPWs do not terminate the underlying obligation but rather prevent the ordinary effects of the breach from materializing. In the ICJ's words, the obligation remains 'dormant' for the duration of the CPW.[5]

The work of the ILC on CPWs was intended to capture the defenses available to States under general international law. Special treaty regimes and self-contained systems may modify these defenses or do away with them (*lex specialis*).[6] The key implication here is that if mistake of fact is found to constitute a CPW, it would, in principle, preclude the wrongfulness of any breach of international law,[7] regardless of its source,[8] except where the special law provides otherwise. This is the question addressed in this chapter.

4.2 Objective Responsibility and Putative Countermeasures

It is a common reality in international life that States may need to react to wrongs committed against them, sometimes without a moment for deliberation. In many cases, mistakes are bound to happen. The question arises then as to how international law deals with measures adopted by a State based on an inaccurate assessment that another State has violated an obligation owed to it. This constellation is referred to in this book by the name of 'putative countermeasures'.

The starting point is, as ever, the obligation of States to resolve their disputes peacefully. Article 33 of the United Nations Charter provides that this duty must be complied with *a fortiori* when an international dispute is 'likely to endanger the maintenance of international peace and security' and provides that the means at States'

---

[3] ICJ (1997), para. 101.

[4] ILC (2001), Commentary to Chapter V of Part One, paras. 3, 4.

[5] For the purposes of this chapter, the distinction becomes apparent when one compares Article 23 of the ILC Articles on State Responsibility with Article 61 of the Vienna Convention on the Law of Treaties. Both cover instances of impossibility, but they have different thresholds and effects. Article 61 of the Vienna Convention requires 'impossibility of performing a treaty … result[ing] from the permanent disappearance or destruction of an object indispensable for the execution of the treaty.' In these cases, Article 61 of the Vienna Convention permits invoking the impossibility as a ground to withdraw from the treaty or otherwise terminate it (if the impossibility is permanent) or to suspend its operation (if the impossibility is temporary).

[6] See Article 55 of the Articles on State Responsibility.

[7] Cf. Paddeu (2012), p. 458.

[8] ILC (2001), General Commentary, para. 4.

disposal include negotiation, enquiry, mediation, conciliation, arbitration, judicial settlement and resort to regional agencies or arrangements. The underlying policy is that States should not do justice with their own hands in circumstances where this may endanger the stability of international relations. The same policy underlies the inherent right to self-defense regulated in Article 51 of the United Nations Charter, which provides that this right is temporary, pending a decision by the United Nations Security Council on the matter.[9] Indeed, measures adopted by States in self-defense must be notified immediately to the Security Council, whose authority and responsibility to take 'such action as it deems necessary in order to maintain or restore international peace and security' shall never be curtailed. Crucially, the right to resort to self-defense operates 'until the Security Council has taken measures necessary to maintain international peace and security'. From these rules of customary and conventional international law, the conclusion suggests itself that unilateral actions by States to vindicate their own rights must be subject to strict conditions to ensure the regularity of international relations.

This understanding is reflected in the secondary norms. Under the ILC's Articles on State Responsibility, the regime of countermeasures is regulated in a detailed manner in Chapter II of Part Three. It is no surprise why Part Three is titled 'the implementation of the international responsibility of a State'. This section regulates how a State can put into operation the rules governing responsibility when it has been aggrieved by an internationally wrongful act. As is evidence by its placement as Chapter I, the primary focus is laid upon the *invocation* of responsibility, which more often than not takes the form of an international claim being brought through the channels recognized by customary international law.[10] This first Chapter addresses who shall be considered an injured State[11]; describes the circumstances under which a State that does not fulfill this condition is entitled to bring a claim anyway[12]; and provides specifics regarding the bringing of an international claim to vindicate the right that has been violated.

Countermeasures are, in this context, regulated as an exceptional course of action to implement the international responsibility of another State. So exceptional in fact, that the Articles on State Responsibility contemplate them as a circumstance that precludes the wrongfulness of a conduct that is otherwise not in conformity with an international obligation.[13] A countermeasure is understood in this context as a conduct that violates international law, but that is undertaken with the purpose of inducing the other State to resume performance of its own obligations.[14] If the measure complies with the requirements laid down in customary international law, it will be considered a lawful mechanism to bring the other violation to an end.

[9] Ruys (2010), p. 58.

[10] ICJ (1949a), p. 177.

[11] See Article 42.

[12] See Article 48.

[13] Article 22 of the Articles on State Responsibility.

[14] Article 49 (1) of the Articles on State Responsibility.

The dangers inherent in this type of action are evident. Indeed, the existence of a rule allowing for countermeasures opens the doors wide for abuse by States that may choose to utilize it as a pretext to dishonor their international obligations. Thus, customary international law imposes on this right a series of safeguards. Countermeasures can only be adopted against a State that has failed to comply with an obligation owed to the first State.[15] Their lawfulness is bound by time, since the State is only allowed to withhold performance for the duration necessary to induce the other State to bring its own conduct into conformity with international law.[16] Moreover, the countermeasure can only be adopted in respect of an obligation that the State taking the measure owes to the original wrongdoer.[17] The countermeasure must be adopted in such a way that it will allow the performance of the obligation to be resumed, circumstances permitting.[18] Before adopting the countermeasure, a warning must be issued to the other State, signaling that this course of action will be taken unless and until the other State resumes performance of its own obligations, offering the possibility to negotiate a settlement.[19] The countermeasure must be suspended if the original wrong ceases or if the dispute has been submitted to a court or tribunal for judicial resolution.[20] Crucially, the countermeasure must be proportionate to the injury suffered.[21] Although these rules apply to non-forcible action,[22] it is worth noting that the use of force in self-defense is also subject under international custom to the requirements of necessity and proportionality.[23]

The question of putative countermeasures is answered in the commentary to the Articles. Particularly, the ILC comments that Article 49 (1) of the Articles on State Responsibility

> ...presupposes an *objective standard* for the taking of countermeasures, and in particular requires that the countermeasure be taken against a State which is responsible for an internationally wrongful act in order to induce that State to comply with its obligations of cessation and reparation. *A State taking countermeasures acts at its peril, if its view of the question of wrongfulness turns out not to be well founded. A State which resorts to countermeasures based on its unilateral assessment of the situation does so at its own risk and may incur responsibility for its own wrongful conduct in the event of an incorrect assessment.*[24]

The idea that a State is responsible for its own erroneous assessments is consistent with the treatment given by the Articles to the nature of international responsibility. If a State's accountability for violating international law is objective as a general

[15] Ibid.

[16] Article 49 (2) of the Articles on State Responsibility.

[17] Ibid.

[18] Article 49 (3) of the Articles on State Responsibility.

[19] Article 52 of the Articles on State Responsibility.

[20] Article 52 (3) of the Articles on State Responsibility.

[21] Article 51 of the Articles on State Responsibility.

[22] Article 50 (1) (*a*) of the Articles on State Responsibility.

[23] ICJ (1986), paras. 176, 194, 237, ICJ (1996), para. 41, ICJ (2003), paras. 51, 68, 73–77, ICJ (2005), para. 147.

[24] ILC (2001), Art. 49, para. 3 (emphasis added).

rule,[25] then preclusion of wrongfulness should also be objective in the same measure. To accept automatically that a State's perception of a given circumstance leads to exoneration would conflict with the idea that, absent a differing provision in the primary rules, international responsibility arises from the objective lack of conformity between a State's actions and the obligations incumbent upon it.[26] The resulting conclusion is that if a countermeasure fails to comply with any of the requirements laid down in customary international law due to a mistake of fact made by the State or its agents, the measure will be wrongful regardless of whether the mistake was reasonable or excusable. The State assumes responsibility for its own decision to resort to unilateral measures to vindicate its rights, for better or for worse. Otherwise, international law would be shifting the burden of proving the wrongfulness onto the State that may not even be acting contrary to international law at all. This rule incentivizes caution and initiative to negotiate to resolve the dispute through established mechanisms instead of breaking international norms. A measure taken in response to an imaginary wrong, against the wrong State or in excess to what was required in light of the situation is considered illegal and attracts international responsibility, regardless of the reasonableness of the mistake of fact that led to it.

To support the idea that the objective existence of an internationally wrongful act is an unavoidable requirement for the taking of countermeasures, the ILC points *inter alia* to the ICJ's Judgment in the *Gabčíkovo-Nagymaros Project* case. In that case, Slovakia argued that Czechoslovakia's decisions to implement Variant C and put it into operation could alternatively be considered a countermeasure taken against Hungary's own illegal conduct, precluding any wrongfulness found by the Court.[27] After finding that Czechoslovakia's implementation of Variant C was in violation of the 1977 Treaty concerning the construction and operation of the Gabčíkovo-Nagymaros System of Locks,[28] the Court turned to the question of countermeasures. It established that under customary law countermeasures must only be adopted 'in response to a previous international wrongful act of another State and must be directed against that State'.[29]

This statement, although elementary in nature (and in full accord with the ILC's codification), is quite significant in the facts of the *Gabčíkovo-Nagymaros Project* case. Indeed, before resorting to the alternative argument of countermeasures, Czechoslovakia and later Slovakia argued that implementing Variant C had been the only viable way to comply with the aims of the 1977 Treaty in light of Hungary's decision to abandon the construction works at Dunakiliti. In their position, implementing Variant C was lawful because it constituted an 'approximate application' of the Treaty's aims,[30] in line with a theory put forward by Judge Sir Hersch Lauterpacht in his separate opinion in the *Admissibility of Hearings of Petitioners by the*

[25] See Chap. 3, Sect. 3.1.

[26] Article 12 of the Articles on State Responsibility.

[27] ICJ (1997), para. 67.

[28] Ibid., para. 78.

[29] Ibid., para. 83.

[30] Ibid., para. 67.

Committee on South West Africa advisory opinion.[31] In effect, Czechoslovakia and Slovakia were arguing that international law conferred upon them a certain measure of discretion in implementing the 1977 Treaty and that Hungary's own unlawful acts forced them to take this route. The Court did not rule on whether this 'principle of approximate application' was a recognizable legal rule, but it did find that any discretion to be found in the implementation of the 1977 Treaty could only be based on the Treaty itself and exercised within the confines of the instrument's own parameters:

> It is not necessary for the Court to determine whether there is a principle of international law or a general principle of law of "approximate application" because, even if such a principle existed, it could by definition only be employed within the limits of the treaty in question. In the view of the Court, Variant C does not meet that cardinal condition with regard to the 1977 Treaty.[32]

This *renvoi* to the primary rule (here the 1977 Treaty) is consistent with the theory of responsibility set out by the ILC in the Articles on State Responsibility.[33] It confirmed that the standard to be applied to the existence of a wrongful act was objective. But in this context, this deceptively simple statement goes a bit further. It confirms that the standard to be applied to Hungary's own illegal act also had to be objective. The Court's statement of the rule regarding the taking of countermeasures thus affirms that Hungary's internationally wrongful act had to be a 'previous' one; in the author's view, this statement in context presupposes objective existence. This is a conclusion that also agrees with the aims of countermeasures and their regulation in international law. The very notion of a countermeasure presupposes the belief of the State taking it that it has been the victim of unlawful action by another State, which violated its rights or interests in some way. The author ventures the guess that this conclusion corresponds to all examples of States taking countermeasures in practice. If a belief (however honest or reasonable) was enough to trigger the permissibility of countermeasures, then the purpose of regulating them in the first place—to prevent abuses in the exercise of unilateral self-help—would vanish. The law needs to impose an objective standard to them. This does not mean that the State cannot, in practice, adopt a countermeasure based on limited evidence or a split-second decision required by the circumstances. It simply means that, if the State makes a mistake, it cannot avoid the duty of repairing the resulting injury by appealing to the urgency of its actions or the sincerity of its intentions.

A crucial element of the ILC's commentary is that this feature of international custom does not apply to countermeasures only. Indeed,

> In this respect, there is no difference between countermeasures and other circumstances precluding wrongfulness.[34]

The idea that the preclusion of wrongfulness requires an objective basis, then, necessarily permeates the exercise of applying the law on CPWs to any set of facts.

---

[31] Ibid., para. 75.

[32] Ibid., para. 76.

[33] See Chap. 3, Sect. 3.1.

[34] ILC (2001), Art. 49, para. 3.

It will also be the starting point of the analysis contained in the subsequent sections of this chapter.

4.3 Mistake of Fact as an Autonomous CPW?

The question of whether a mistake of fact would qualify as an independent CPW arose indirectly in the *Land and Maritime Boundary* case before the ICJ. In 1994, Cameroon instituted proceedings requesting the ICJ to declare that sovereignty over Bakassi Peninsula and Lake Chad belonged to it, and that Nigeria's governmental and military presence in these areas was inconsistent with international law. One of Nigeria's main counterarguments was that its presence in and administration of Bakassi Peninsula and Lake Chad resulted from having made the 'honest and reasonable mistake' of believing that it had sovereignty over those areas. This case gives ample opportunity to discuss the existence and content of a potential defense based on mistake in territorial matters.

The analysis starts with the characterization of the mistake defense in Nigeria's pleadings:

> As Nigeria has noted above ... one of the conditions to be satisfied before a State incurs international responsibility for its conduct is that the conduct complained of must not fall within certain accepted justifications. In that context Nigeria invoked honest belief, reasonable mistake and self-defense as justifications for a number of the incidents relied on by Cameroon.[35]

By placing mistake on par with self-defense (which the ILC Articles consider a CPW under Article 21), Nigeria implies that the theory of mistake of fact is an independent CPW. Indeed, the respondent State did not raise this argument under the rubric of any other justification. In that sense, although the ILC's work on State responsibility had not yet been concluded at the time, the CPWs in the 1996 draft Articles were generally identical to those in the final codification, meaning that mistakes of fact were not expressly listed as an autonomous defense. This absence was the basis of one of Cameroon's counterarguments:

> There are six circumstances that preclude wrongfulness, no more and no less, and this is the result of a discussion that has lasted for many years, as those on the other side of the bar are perfectly well aware. Thus there is no hint of reasonable mistake or honest belief, either in the draft or, despite what Nigeria implies, in its preparatory works . . .[36]

Understood as the invocation of mistake as a CPW, Nigeria's argument raised the question whether the list of CPWs codified in the ILC Articles is exhaustive. The commentary to the Articles certainly implies that it is. In the words of the Commission, the codification 'sets out the circumstances precluding wrongfulness

[35] Nigeria (2001), para. 15.54.

[36] ICJ Verbatim Record 2002/2007, p. 27, para. 33.

presently recognized under general international law.'[37] Other candidates, like the defense of *non adimpleti contractus*, were rejected.[38] It is notable that the process of codifying the issue of CPWs was one of progressive discovery. Prior to the start of the ILC's work, the 1930 Hague Conference, convened with the purpose of codifying international law, identified two circumstances under which States could decline their responsibility: cases where the act 'was occasioned by the immediate necessity of self-defense' or occurred 'in circumstances justifying the exercise of reprisals'.[39]

The concept of defenses, including force majeure and necessity, was introduced to the ILC's work on the subject by Special Rapporteur Francisco García-Amador in his First Report on State Responsibility.[40] This Report also considered other defenses that are not CPWs in the 2001 codification, such as extinctive prescription.[41] García-Amador's Third Report included contributory negligence by the aggrieved alien as a circumstance exonerating the State; and all three defenses (force majeure, necessity and contribution by the alien) could potentially operate as mitigating circumstances should they be inadmissible as grounds for exoneration.[42] The Eighth Report on State Responsibility by Special Rapporteur Roberto Ago addressed once again the issue, contemplating as defenses (except now using the term 'circumstances precluding wrongfulness') consent, 'legitimate application of a sanction', force majeure, fortuitous event, necessity and self-defense.[43] Thus, while the list of CPWs may well have been intended to be exhaustive, this of course does not rule out subsequent developments in customary international law.

The Parties' remarks in this case also raise questions as to the nature of the mistake defense. The complications arising from the distinction between justifications and excuses[44] are showcased in the Parties' pleadings. When describing its mistake defense, Nigeria initially phrased it in terms, not of a justification, but of an excuse based on fault:

> There is no established rule of customary international law that international responsibility is in all cases absolute. It is more in accordance with State and international judicial practice for international responsibility in appropriate cases to be essentially based on fault, requiring either intentional or negligent conduct on the part of the State if it is to be held internationally responsible for that conduct.[45]

---

[37] ILC (2001), Commentary to Chapter V of Part One, para. 9.

[38] Ibid.

[39] Amador (1956), pp. 224–225.

[40] Ibid., pp. 208–209, paras. 183–191.

[41] Ibid., pp. 208–209, paras. 183–191.

[42] Amador (1958), p. 50, Arts. 13–14.

[43] Ago (1979), pp. 27–66, paras. 48–153. Ago's Eighth Report appears to conceive of distress as a subclass of force majeure.

[44] See Sect. 4.4.2.

[45] Nigeria (1999), para. 24.34.

Nigeria later described its mistake as a 'justification',[46] a ground that serves to 'preclude international responsibility'.[47] In some instances, however, Nigeria described its mistake as *both* a circumstance that excludes the violation of the primary rule ('l'erreur raisonnable qui accompagne un acte exclut qu'il y ait violation de ladite règle') *and*, alternatively, as a CPW in case a violation indeed occurs ('s'il y a bel et bien eu violation, l'existence de l'erreur raisonnable constituera une circonstance excluant l'illicéité de l'acte').[48] This ambivalence may be explained by the fact that Nigeria treated the theory of mistake as an independent defense, which raises two problems. The first is a problem of evidence since Nigeria at no point provides the basis for the defense's existence under customary international law. The second is that the claim that this defense operates at two levels (primary and secondary) conflicts with the theory of objective responsibility that is well established in custom,[49] and gives rise to potential redundancy. This confusion is further complicated by Nigeria's argument that the case did not implicate Article 2 (4) of the Charter, since Nigeria did not cross an internationally recognized boundary by force.[50]

How did the ICJ make sense of this complexity? The Court settled the dispute by first defining the boundary between the two States and ordering each one to evacuate the other's territory as determined in the Judgment:

> ...[Nigeria] further contends that, even if the Court should find that Cameroon has sovereignty over these areas, the Nigerian presence there was the result of a 'reasonable mistake' or 'honest belief'. Accordingly, Nigeria cannot be held internationally responsible for conduct which, at the time it took place, Nigeria had every reason to believe was lawful...
>
> The Court notes that Nigeria is under an obligation in the present case expeditiously and without condition to withdraw its administration and its military and police forces from that area of Lake Chad which falls within Cameroon's sovereignty and from the Bakassi Peninsula...
>
> The Court further observes that Cameroon is under an obligation expeditiously and without condition to withdraw any administration or military or police forces which may be present in areas along the land boundary from Lake Chad to the Bakassi Peninsula which pursuant to the present Judgment fall within the sovereignty of Nigeria. Nigeria has the same obligation in regard to any administration or military or police forces which may be present in areas along the land boundary from Lake Chad to the Bakassi Peninsula which pursuant to the present Judgment fall within the sovereignty of Cameroon...[51]

The ICJ's Judgment in this respect does not provide a clear answer as to the correctness of Nigeria's mistake defense. An argument supporting the efficaciousness of the mistake could point out that the ICJ determined the States' respective territories but did not expressly apportion responsibility. Indeed, Nigeria made this argument relying on a similar attitude adopted by the ICJ in the *Temple of Preah Vihear* case:

---

[46] Nigeria (2001), para. 15.54.

[47] Nigeria (1999), para. 24.34.

[48] ICJ Verbatim Record 2002/2020, para. 23.

[49] See Chap. 3, Sect. 3.1.

[50] This argument, reminiscent of the requirement of an '*animus aggressionis*' in the context of Article 2 (4) of the Charter, will be addressed in Sect. 4.6.2.

[51] ICJ (2002), paras. 311, 314, 315.

> ... the Parties did not seek, and the Court did not adjudge, any finding of international responsibility as against the other party should it be held not to have sovereignty over the area in dispute: the Parties, and the Court, limited themselves to certain specific matters such as the return of property and the withdrawal of official personnel.[52]

Additionally, Nigeria made the argument that, unless and until the ICJ determined the exact location of its boundary with Cameroon, its mistake would continue to operate. Having determined the boundary, the ICJ referred to *Temple of Preah Vihear* to reason its decision that both Cameroon and Nigeria had coextensive obligations to withdraw from the other's territory as declared by the Court.[53] Under this reasoning, this attitude would imply that Nigeria's mistake of fact exonerated it from responsibility for its administration of Cameroon's territory, but once the boundary dispute was settled by the ICJ, the obligation was born for Nigeria immediately to withdraw. If Nigeria failed to do so, it would no longer be shielded by its mistake (which had already been dissipated by the ICJ) and would therefore incur international responsibility.

However, the ICJ's ambiguous treatment of Nigeria's mistake argument could easily be used to support the opposite conclusion. The Court never identifies Nigeria's mistake as a key aspect underpinning its decision. In fact, after recapitulating Nigeria's position as to mistake, the ICJ goes on immediately to order both parties to withdraw. The Court's focus on the delimitation aspect can be traced back to the language of Cameroon's Application instituting proceedings: Cameroon described the dispute as relating 'essentially' to the sovereignty over the disputed territories, since delimitation had 'remained a partial one,' 'despite many attempts to complete it'.[54] Cameroon asked the ICJ to determine its boundary with Nigeria to 'avoid further incidents between the two countries'.[55]

Moreover, the comparison to *Temple of Preah Vihear* is not useful, since in that case Cambodia did not request the ICJ to declare responsibility or order reparations against Thailand.[56] In contrast, Cameroon did ask the ICJ to declare that the Respondent's acts 'involve the responsibility of [Nigeria]' and that 'consequently, and on account of the material and non-material damage inflicted upon [Cameroon], reparation ... is due'.[57] And the ICJ did make a pronouncement regarding responsibility:[58]

> Cameroon, however, is not only asking the Court for an end to Nigeria's administrative and military presence in Cameroonian territory but also for guarantees of non-repetition in the future. Such submissions are undoubtedly admissible ... However, the Judgment delivered today specifies in definitive and mandatory terms the land and maritime boundary between the two States. With all uncertainty dispelled in this regard, the Court cannot envisage a situation

---

52 Nigeria (2001), para. 15.57 (1).

53 ICJ (2002), paras. 313–315.

54 Ibid., para. 1.

55 Ibid., paras. 1–3.

56 ICJ (1962), pp. 9–11.

57 ICJ (2002), para. 25, clauses (*e′*) and (*e″*).

58 Ibid., para. 318 (italics in the original).

> where either Party, after withdrawing its military and police Forces and administration from the other's territory, would fail to respect the territorial sovereignty of that Party. Hence Cameroon's submissions on this point cannot be upheld...

In a similar fashion as it did in *Corfu Channel*,[59] the ICJ went on to declare that the Judgment itself made good the injury suffered by Cameroon:

> In the circumstances of the case, the Court considers moreover that, by the very fact of the present Judgment and of the evacuation of the Cameroonian territory occupied by Nigeria, the injury suffered by Cameroon by reason of the occupation of its territory will in all events have been sufficiently addressed. The Court will not therefore seek to ascertain whether and to what extent Nigeria's responsibility to Cameroon has been engaged as a result of that occupation...[60]

Therefore, the argument would go that the ICJ did assign responsibility for the occupation of Lake Chad and Bakassi Peninsula, but it simply rejected Cameroon's requested form of reparation. This attitude would presuppose the existence of international responsibility, even if not explicitly.

In the author's opinion, it is difficult to draw many conclusions for the theory of mistake of fact from the ICJ's reasoning in this case. Following any of these two lines of argumentation would risk reading too much into the Judgment. Crucially, appraising the ICJ's reasoning through the lens of the theory of mistake of fact, it becomes clear that the case truly concerns a mistake of *law*. Indeed, Nigeria's argument does not challenge the fact that its agents were present in Lake Chad or Bakassi Peninsula. Rather, the case concerns a mistake regarding the position of the international border between Cameroon and Nigeria, which in truth relates not to the land, air or sea themselves, but to the litigating States' rights over them. These arise as a matter of international law. And as will be discussed below, international law generally rejects this kind of mistake.[61] Therefore, the author concludes this case does not demonstrate the existence of an autonomous CPW of mistake of fact.

4.4 Force Majeure and Distress

4.4.1 Introduction

The commentary to the ILC Articles discusses instances of 'accidental' and erroneous violations of international law in the unlikeliest of places: as part of its commentary on the doctrine of force majeure under Article 23. This provision describes force majeure as

> ...the occurrence of an irresistible force or of an unforeseen event, beyond the control of the State, making it materially impossible in the circumstances to perform the obligation.

59 ICJ (1949b), p. 35.

60 ICJ (2002), para. 319.

61 See Sect. 4.4.1.

The ILC's commentary appears to accept without much debate that instances of 'accidental' breaches of international law fall within the purview of Article 23 of the Articles, so long as the accident was unavoidable. For instance, the ILC exemplifies this form of force majeure stating that

> ...cases of material impossibility have occurred, e.g. where a State aircraft is forced, due to damage or loss of control of the aircraft owing to weather, into the airspace of another State without the latter's authorization.[62]

The inclusion of these cases within Article 23 of the Articles on State Responsibility may be somewhat startling when considering the doctrine of force majeure from a domestic perspective. Generally, this doctrine covers cases where performance has become objectively impossible due to an unforeseeable and unavoidable impediment.[63] The kind of impossibility contemplated by the norm varies from system to system. In some jurisdictions, the norm regulates cases where the purpose of the obligation has become frustrated by a supervening event.[64] Some systems distinguish between force majeure and other impediments, like the *théorie de l'imprévision*, impracticability and hardship, where the obligation becomes too onerous or worthless, albeit not impossible.[65] At the private international level, these doctrines are discussed in the context of international contracts,[66] especially those for the sale of goods.[67] Of course, the efficacy of the force majeure defense, most often discussed in the context of contracts, largely depends on the extent to which the jurisdiction adopts the theory of fault; the larger the incidence of fault, the more flexible the force majeure defense will be, as it gives the debtor more latitude to disclaim responsibility based on his or her awareness of the facts and intention to harm.[68] But the general rule is that actual and objective impossibility is required to avoid liability.[69]

In the State responsibility context, the rejection of fault as a general element for wrongful acts[70] should lead to a stricter concept of force majeure. Yet, it appears that the ILC codification goes the opposite way. The definitions provided by the ILC suggest that the law of State responsibility conceives of force majeure as a circumstance that makes the breach of international law unavoidable, and not necessarily

---

[62] ILC (2001), Art. 23, para. 5.

[63] Schwenzer et al. (2012), para. 45.33; Article 79 (1) of the United Nations Convention on Contracts for the International Sale of Goods (1980), Article 7.1.7 of the UNIDROIT Principles on International Commercial Contracts.

[64] Schwenzer et al. (2012), para. 45.29.

[65] Ibid., paras. 45.99–45.106.

[66] For instance, Articles 6.2.1–6.2.3 and 7.1.7 of the Principles on International Commercial Contracts, 2016, developed by the Institut International pour l'Unification du Droit Privé (UNIDROIT).

[67] Article 79 of the United Nations Convention on Contracts for the International Sale of Goods.

[68] Schwenzer et al. (2012), para. 45.01.

[69] Ibid., para. 45.33.

[70] See Chap. 3, Sect. 3.1.

one that makes performance impossible.[71] In a similar vein, the United Nations Secretariat's study on the subject defines force majeure as follows:

> "Force majeure" has been defined, *lato sensu*, as an unforeseen or foreseen but inevitable or irresistible event external to the obligor which makes it impossible for him to perform the obligation concerned.[72]

This crucial difference, albeit subtle, is no accident; it is not only supported by State practice but can also be traced back to previous drafts of the ILC Articles.

In his 1979 Eighth Report on State Responsibility, Special Rapporteur Roberto Ago included separate draft provisions for force majeure and 'fortuitous events'. While force majeure (draft Article 31) covered instances of absolute impossibility, the concept of fortuitous event was framed in the following terms in draft Article 32:

> The international wrongfulness of an act of a State not in conformity with what is required of it by an international obligation is precluded if, owing to a supervening external and unforeseeable factor, it is impossible for the author of the conduct attributable to the State to realize that its conduct is not in conformity with the international obligation.[73]

This distinction traces back to arguments advanced by some scholars that associated force majeure with irresistibility and *cas fortuit* with unpredictability.[74] By its wording, the 1979 draft Articles would regulate true instances of mistake of fact and of law ('impossible for the author of the conduct attributable to the State to realize that its conduct is not in conformity with the international obligation'). This definition, which as has been pointed out before does not correspond to the ordinary understanding of the domestic concept of *cas fortuit*,[75] had four salient features. The first is that it described how the mistake of fact would be formed: it needed to affect the author whose conduct was attributable to the State. In other words, the error by the State agent would translate to *cas fortuit* for the State if the remaining conditions were met. The second is that this draft provision, like Article 23 of the 2001 Articles on State Responsibility, would require a catalyst event, ruling out spontaneous mistakes. The third is that this trigger event needed to be 'supervening'; in other words, initial mistakes as to the circumstances surrounding performance of the obligation would not be covered.[76] Finally, this draft provision would require the catalyst event to be 'unforeseeable', while current Article 23 uses the language 'unforeseen'. This could point to a shift in the degree of foreseeability required to invoke a provision: the term 'unforeseen' would only require that the obligor did not anticipate, in fact, the catalyst event. In contrast, the term 'unforeseeable' would require the event to be unpredictable from the perspective of a reasonable third person. Mere lack of

---

[71] See generally ILC (2001), Art. 23, paras. 1–5.

[72] ILC (1978), p. 69, para. 13 (italics in the original, footnotes removed).

[73] Ago (1979), p. 66.

[74] ILC (1978), p. 70, para. 19.

[75] Szurek (2010), p. 476.

[76] In this respect, modern international law may regulate initial mistakes within the concept of 'error' in the law of treaties, Article 48 of the Vienna Convention on the Law of Treaties.

anticipation would not suffice. As is explained below, the 2001 ILC Articles appear to adopt an intermediate position.[77]

In the 1996 draft Articles, these two concepts were brought together into a single provision, draft Article 31 ('Force majeure and fortuitous events'):

> The wrongfulness of an act of a State not in conformity with an international obligation of that State is precluded if the act was due to an irresistible force or to an unforeseen external event beyond its control which made it materially impossible for the State to act in conformity with that obligation or to know that its conduct was not in conformity with that obligation.[78]

In reviewing this provision in his Second Report on State Responsibility, Special Rapporteur James Crawford acknowledged the potential of draft Article 31 to cover instances of mistake:

> One of the curious features of article 31 is the phrase 'made it materially impossible … to know that its conduct was not in conformity with that obligation'. This suggests that State responsibility depends on the State 'knowing' that its conduct is wrongful, yet in general such knowledge is not required. *Ignorance of a State's legal obligations is no excuse for breaching them, nor is mistake of law. It is true that there might be an innocent mistake of fact (e.g. as to the location of an aircraft, owing to an undetected fault in navigational equipment), and this might qualify as a circumstance precluding wrongfulness. . .*[79]

Special Rapporteur Crawford went on to make the most significant observation in this context:

> ... Article 31 can, however, be formulated without the introduction of overtly subjective elements: it should only apply in cases where an unforeseen external event deprived a State from having knowledge of a fact which was an essential element of its responsibility *in the circumstances*, and without which the conduct in question would not have been wrongful. On this basis the reference in article 31 to knowledge of wrongfulness can be deleted.[80]

Thus, Special Rapporteur Crawford removed the reference to 'knowledge of wrongfulness' in draft Article 31; moreover, following a comment by France, Crawford removed the reference to 'fortuitous event' to prevent redundancy,[81] leaving the provision largely as it is today. Despite these changes, Crawford's understanding of draft Article 31 as covering mistakes of fact was carried over to the final codification. It is clear from the previously cited passages that the purpose of collapsing force majeure and fortuitous event into a single provision and removing the 'overtly subjective elements' was to rule out mistakes of *law*. It also shows that some mistakes of *fact* were intended to be retained as a manifestation of force majeure. Article 23 of the final Articles on State Responsibility indicates that a situation of force majeure, as understood under that provision, can be caused by *either* 'an irresistible force' *or* 'an

---

[77] See Sect. 4.4.8.

[78] ILC (1996), p. 61.

[79] Crawford (1999), p. 66, para. 262 (footnotes removed and emphasis added).

[80] Ibid. (emphasis in the original).

[81] As described by the United Nations Secretariat's study of 1978, both notions (force majeure, *stricto sensu* and fortuitous event) fall within a broader concept of force majeure in the State responsibility context. ILC (1978), p. 70, para. 19.

unforeseen event', so long as either alternative makes it materially impossible for the State to perform the international obligation. The ILC's description of the elements of Article 23 itself suggests that these two occurrences are alternative.[82] This traces back to draft Articles 31 and 32 of Ago's Eighth Report, where unforeseen events were associated with *cas fortuit*, which in turn covered instances of mistake of fact. The coverage of mistakes of fact under Article 23 is confirmed by the inclusion of the language 'in the circumstances', which was not part of the 1996 draft Article 31 (1). Special Rapporteur Crawford explains, in the above-cited passage of its Second Report on State Responsibility, that this term is intended to capture some instances of mistake of fact without having to include 'overtly subjective elements'. This is confirmed in the Second Report itself, where it is pointed out that

> As originally drafted, paragraph 1 also covered cases of force majeure which made it impossible for the State "to know that its conduct was not in conformity with" the obligation. This added a confusing subjective element and appeared to contradict the principle that ignorance of wrongfulness (i.e. ignorance of law) is not an excuse. The words were intended to cover cases such as an unforeseen failure of navigational equipment causing an aircraft to intrude on the airspace of another State. The words "in the circumstances" are intended to cover this situation without the need to refer to knowledge of wrongfulness (see paragraph 262 above).[83]

Therefore, the drafting of Article 23 of the ILC Articles on State Responsibility reveals that some instances of mistake of fact are covered by the concept of force majeure under international law. The requirements for such mistakes to fall under Article 23 will be covered later in this chapter.

4.4.2 *Excuses, Justifications and Mistakes of Fact*

From a theoretical perspective, one needs to distinguish between 'justifications' and 'excuses'.[84] Each concept addresses a separate aspect of wrongfulness from a legal perspective. A justification attacks the illegal character itself: its effect is classifying the conduct as 'lawful' even if it conflicts with other rules in the legal system. This is because a conduct falling within a ground for justification will be taken to safeguard a legal interest that the system perceives as more important than the infringed rule. Thus, for instance, if a father steals bread to feed his starving children, the law may attenuate his responsibility because the inherent value of life outweighs the protection of property in the individual case. In contrast, an excuse does not negate the illegality of the conduct, but only exculpates the actor due to his or her special circumstances. The act is still regarded as wrongful, but the law chooses to impose no culpability.

---

[82] ILC (2001), Art. 23, para. 2. Note that this interpretation is not unanimous: Szurek (2010), p. 477.

[83] Crawford (1999), p. 88, Art. 31, para. 2.

[84] Austin (1956), p. 2, Berman (2003), p. 4.

The ILC itself recognizes that national practice on defenses is not uniform and attempts to develop an independent theory.[85] As evidenced by the start of this chapter, the language used to describe CPWs is reminiscent of justifications.[86] The name itself shows that the consequence of successfully invoking a CPW is wiping out the wrongfulness of the act. In contrast, the ILC's codification does not generally recognize excuses in the State responsibility context, despite the objections of many academics.[87] The distinction can be confirmed by reference to the preparatory works of the ILC Articles. In its Report on the work of the 25th Session, the ILC explained that

> ... For the time being, in the Commission's view, it is only necessary to say that the true effect of the presence of such circumstances [precluding wrongfulness] is not, at least in the normal case, to preclude responsibility that would otherwise result from an act wrongful in itself, but rather to preclude the characterization of the conduct of the State in one of those circumstances as wrongful . . .[88]

Special Rapporteur Roberto Ago's Eighth Report on State Responsibility refers to this paragraph when explaining the selection of the term 'circumstances precluding *wrongfulness*' (as opposed to 'circumstances precluding *responsibility*'):

> ... we are firmly of the view that it would be incorrect to regard the expressions "circumstances precluding responsibility" and "circumstances precluding wrongfulness" as mere synonyms. Such an idea could be considered valid only by those who define a wrongful act in terms of the responsibility resulting from that act or, to put it more plainly, who characterize an act as wrongful only because the law attaches responsibility to the act in question ... However, matters appear differently to those who regard the notion of the "wrongful act" as a notion which, although linked to that of "responsibility" nevertheless remains distinct from it. Throughout the draft articles, the Commission has made clear its conviction that a distinction must be drawn between the idea of wrongfulness, expressing the fact that certain conduct by a State conflicts with an obligation imposed on that State by a "primary" rule of international law, and the idea of responsibility, indicating the legal consequences which another, "secondary" rule of international law attaches to the act of the State that such conduct consists of . . .[89]

The discussion as to the relationship between the wrongfulness of conduct (i.e. the incompatibility with a rule of international law) and the responsibility that results from it is central to the idea of justifications and excuses. The line drawn by Ago and the ILC in the cited passages indicates that the CPWs do not simply shield the State from responsibility, but have a deeper effect: to classify the appraised conduct as no longer internationally unlawful. The preclusion of responsibility comes as a byproduct of the preclusion of wrongfulness.[90] Therefore, CPW fit more exactly

---

[85] ILC (2001), Commentary to Chapter V of Part One, para. 7.

[86] Note, however, that the term is not used consistently in the ILC's commentary: CPWs are described as 'provid[ing] a *justification or excuse* for non-performance while the circumstance in question subsists' (emphasis added). ILC (2001), Commentary to Chapter V of Part One, para. 2.

[87] Kutoroff (2016), pp. 201–208, Lowe (1999).

[88] ILC (1973), p. 176, Art. 1, para. 12.

[89] Ago (1979), pp. 27–28, para. 50.

[90] Ibid.

within the concept of justifications (which reclassify the conduct as lawful) rather than excuses (which preserve the illegality but preclude the imposition of responsibility).

Mistakes of fact do not fit neatly within the category of justifications. When a person acts based on a mistake of fact, the act is objectively not committed to further a greater good; the law only exculpates the wrongdoer on account of his or her ignorance of the underlying facts. The difficulty is that a person that acts based on mistake *believes* that his or her conduct protects a legal interest of greater importance, as otherwise the mistake theory would fail to exculpate him or her.[91] Although the ILC's commentary does not solve this theoretical problem expressly, the answer may lie with the underlying rationale of force majeure: the law cannot force a State to perform what is impossible (*impossibilium nulla obligatio est*). This higher legal interest may trump the wrongfulness of the conduct when the mistake of fact produces a situation of material impossibility of performance; this is perhaps why the ILC Articles interpret mistakes of fact as circumstances falling under Article 23. Any situation where the mistake does not fulfil the requirements for force majeure would not disclaim the State's responsibility, at least under general international law.

4.4.3 Mistake of Fact Leading to Material Impossibility

The central element of the force majeure exception—impossibility of performance—may at first glance conflict with the idea of mistake as an impediment to performance. An examination of the ILC's codification history will reveal that the concept of force majeure has received a wide range of definitions that differ as to the actual scope of the exception. On the one hand, the concept is linked to a situation of actual and objective impossibility: the ILC's commentary defines force majeure as 'a situation where the State in question is in effect compelled to act in a manner not in conformity with the requirements of an international obligation'[92]; an event that is 'causally linked to the situation of material impossibility'[93]; as well as the use of 'duress or coercion involving force'.[94] This definition is supported by international jurisprudence, including, for example, the *Rainbow Warrior* case.[95] However, broader definitions associate the force majeure concept with that of fault. For instance, the United Nations Secretariat's study on force majeure and fortuitous events points out that

> ...Underlining the close interconnexion that force majeure bears to the degree of diligence an obligor is expected to exercise in each specific legal relationship, force majeure has also been defined in a negative or separative way as an occurrence which is not attributable to

---

[91] Klamberg (2017), p. 331.

[92] ILC (2001), Art. 23, para. 1.

[93] Ibid., Art. 23, para. 2.

[94] Ibid., Art. 23, para. 3; on coercion as force majeure, see Paddeu (2012), p. 397.

[95] Arbitral Tribunal (1990), p. 253.

> any "fault" (*dolus* or culpable negligence) on the part of the obligor, or which takes place independently of the obligor's will and in a manner uncontrollable by him, which makes it impossible to perform the obligation.[96]

In the same vein, the ILC's commentary highlights the fact that force majeure involves the conduct that is 'involuntary or at least involves no element of free choice'.[97] Relevant to the subject of this chapter, force majeure at the international level has also been associated with instances of 'blameless error'.[98]

The reading of Article 23 of the ILC Articles permitting the invocation of mistakes, however, should not be equated to the concept of fault. Article 23 does not render all international obligations dependent on misconduct, lack of due diligence or fault on the part of the State. Rather, the provision relates to actual and objective impossibility resulting from excusable ignorance or misappreciation of the facts. This provision then covers circumstances where the knowledge of a particular fact was a 'material' or physical precondition for the State's conduct, not where a particular mental state was incorporated into the primary rule. The fact that Article 23 only covers cases where the material impossibility is linked to an external event (be it an 'irresistible force' or an 'unforeseen event') serves to reinforce this point, since it means that a mistake of fact, alone and in a vacuum, is insufficient to insulate the State from responsibility. In other words, Article 23 regulates cases where the mistake of fact results from an external event and constitutes a physical impediment for the State's ability to perform the international obligation.

Take, for example, a case where a State has a treaty obligation to accord protection to a vehicle carrying an important artifact. The State then fails to perform this obligation because of a technical malfunction, not attributable to it, which prevents it from knowing of the presence of the artifact in the vehicle in question, or about the location of the vehicle itself. Whether the State's ignorance (or mistake) precludes the wrongfulness of the conduct under Article 23 will depend on the fulfilment of the remaining force majeure requirements, as will be elaborated upon later in this chapter. This is not to say, however, that the treaty obligation in question required the State to have a specific mental state at the moment of the failure to perform; rather, the State's ignorance, caused by a circumstance not attributable to it, constituted an obstacle to its performance of the treaty that may, in the right circumstances, be defensible under Article 23 of the Articles on State Responsibility.

4.4.4 Force Majeure Incorporated into the Primary Rule

The Articles on State Responsibility regulate the force majeure exception as a CPW. However, the documents leading to the 2001 version of the Articles,[99] as well as

[96] ILC (1978), p. 69, para. 13 (italics in the original, footnotes removed).

[97] ILC (2001), Art. 23, para. 1.

[98] Von der Heydte (1958), p. 314.

[99] See e.g. ILC (1978), p. 66, para. 6.

the commentary itself,[100] point out that in some instances the exception is codified at the primary rule level.[101] The difference is important since it determines whether the force majeure event affects the establishment of the wrongful act (Article 2) or precludes responsibility for it (Article 23). If the primary rule is defined by reference to force majeure (as is, for example, Article 44 (4) of the Vienna Convention on Diplomatic Relations, 1961), then such doctrine helps define the contours of the international obligation. As a matter of legal logic, then, these obligations are not susceptible to the application of Article 23, since if an internationally wrongful act has occurred, the force majeure exception has already failed.[102]

Another issue that arises from the dual nature of force majeure is whether the concept, as elaborated upon by the ILC in the Articles on State Responsibility, has equivalent content to the force majeure exceptions defined at the primary rule level. As a starting point, the relevant provision needs to be interpreted by reference to its context and the object and purpose of the treaty,[103] meaning that the scope of the force majeure exception will be informed by the instrument in which it is contained. However, in accordance with the principle of systemic integration, the provision in question needs to be interpreted also by reference to its international normative context,[104] including customary international law.[105] Since the ILC's concept of force majeure is customary,[106] the interpretation of the force majeure provision in the treaty, even if not identical to Article 23, needs to be informed by the ILC's understanding of the concept, as observed from the practice of States.

4.4.5 Putative Force Majeure

What can be distilled from the observations already made is that instances of 'putative force majeure', as it were, are not covered by Article 23 of the ILC Articles. This notion would cover cases in which the State *believes* that performing the obligation is impossible. The discussions leading up to Article 23 as well as the State practice confirm that this situation is not accounted for under general international law as an exception to wrongfulness. Instead, Article 23 would cover only situations in which a misapprehension of a fact physically prevents the State from performing the obligation (occasioning 'material impossibility'). The consequence of this distinction is that in cases of 'putative force majeure' the general rule applies: responsibility is

[100] ILC (2001), Art. 23, para. 6.

[101] See e.g. Sect. 4.4.7.

[102] Cf. Article 55 of the Articles on State Responsibility.

[103] Article 31 (1) of the Vienna Convention on the Law of Treaties.

[104] Article 31 (3) (*c*) of the Vienna Convention on the Law of Treaties.

[105] Koskenniemi (2006), p. 233, para. 462.

[106] Piéri (2021), para. 6.

objective, and a mistake as to the practicability of performance falls within the State's sphere of risk. A breach of international law in these circumstances constitutes an internationally wrongful act and the content of responsibility suffers no alteration.

4.4.6 Accidents and Putative Distress

The examples of erroneous overflight by aircraft show the closeness that exists between force majeure and the CPW of distress, which is codified in Article 24 of the ILC Articles on State Responsibility. This provision reads as follows:

> The wrongfulness of an act of a State not in conformity with an international obligation of that State is precluded if the author of the act in question has no other reasonable way, in a situation of distress, of saving the author's life or the lives of other persons entrusted to the author's care.

This provision addresses 'the specific case where an individual whose acts are attributable to the State is in a situation of peril, either personally or in relation to persons under his or her care' and has no other way of saving life than breaching an international obligation.[107] The ILC explains that cases of distress more often involve aircraft or vessels infringing upon the airspace or waters of another State 'under stress of weather or following mechanical or navigational failure.'[108] Yet, when offering examples that this is so, the ILC refers to a study conducted by the United Nations Secretariat on the practice of States relating to cases of force majeure and fortuitous events.[109] The ILC then elaborates on the relationship between force majeure under Article 23 and distress under Article 24: while in cases of force majeure the State is deprived of any choice due to an external event, in cases of distress the choice remains theoretically possible, albeit 'nullified' by the peril faced by the State's agent.[110] This is the reason why some authors refer to distress as 'relative' impossibility.[111] This description by the ILC presupposes that Article 23 covers cases of 'absolute' impossibility, where the State is deprived of all choice. But any degree of observation is sufficient to blur the distinction. If an aircraft crosses into foreign airspace by accident due to an unexpected storm, is this a case of 'absolute' or 'relative' impossibility? It is no wonder that the ILC itself points out that '[i]t is not always clear whether these cases are based on distress or force majeure.'[112]

Thus, the author believes that it is important to make some observations on the distinction between these two institutions of customary international law. The key difference between them is the entity that suffers the exceptional situation that triggers

---

[107] ILC (2001), Art. 24, para. 1.

[108] Ibid.

[109] Ibid, footnotes 361, 345.

[110] Ibid., para. 1.

[111] Ibid., footnote 360.

[112] Ibid., Art. 23 footnote 351.

their application. While distress concerns a peril suffered only by the State agent, force majeure regulates a situation of impossibility that affects the State machinery more generally. Moreover, distress addresses the individual circumstances of the agent, which justifies a lower standard. The breach does not need to derive from material impossibility but, rather, it suffices that the conduct was the only 'reasonable way' of averting the threat to life. This is the reason why some authors describe distress as a subspecies of necessity, noting that its characteristic notes do not create a distinction in kind.[113]

However, more to the point, there is a key distinction that impacts the State practice related to the theory of mistake of fact. Within the constellation of cases involving aerial intruders, some examples involve a pilot that decides to cross into unauthorized airspace to save her own life or the lives of others, faced with the stress of weather or mechanical malfunctions that endanger the integrity of the aircraft in some way. These are not situations of mistake of fact, properly speaking, but rather situations of distress, because they usually concern a real threat to the life of the tripulants. The pilot is *aware* that she is infringing the aerial space of another State but is forced to do it anyway because the need to safeguard life prevails. This is to be distinguished from cases in which the atmospheric conditions or the failure of navigational equipment prevent the pilot from realizing that she has crossed into unauthorized airspace. This would be the archetypical example of a mistake of fact falling under the definition of force majeure because an external force (the stress of weather or the malfunctioning of navigational equipment) has prevented the State's agent from acquiring knowledge that was a precondition for performing the obligation, in a way that the machinery of the agent's State cannot remedy in the circumstances. In effect, a situation of material impossibility ensues.

The reason these two cases are sometimes lumped together in surveys of State practice is because in both cases, the straying aircraft's conduct is not wrongful. The difference is that one category of cases involves a mistake of fact, and the other does not. Consequently, one would fall under Article 23 of the ILC Articles, and the other may, in the right conditions, be justified according to the CPW of distress.

What stands to the eye in this respect is that many cases of distress do not involve mistakes of fact but are rather 'accidents' in the full sense of the word. The question that arises from this is whether international law would accept as a CPW a situation in which a plea of distress is based on a mistake of fact as understood in this book (i.e. a situation of 'putative distress', in which the agent incorrectly believes that her life or the lives of persons under her care are in danger). This concern may be especially pressing when dealing with law enforcement acts that result in the use of lethal force by mistake, such as the ones examined in the previous chapter.[114] Indeed, the State's law enforcement agent may genuinely and reasonably believe that she or a person under her care is in danger, forcing her to act. However, as the international practice

---

113 Paddeu (2012), p. 462.

114 See Chap. 3, Sect. 3.2.2.

shows, these situations often result in the State's responsibility being triggered. The author believes that a plea of 'putative distress' is not a viable argument in cases involving the use of lethal force for the reasons that follow.

First, in most cases a situation of distress needs to be actually (and not putatively) established, as is shown by the practice cited by the ILC in its commentary to Article 24,[115] as well as the general policy concern that grounds for exoneration should not be too readily accessible in cases of lethal force. The general approach of the ILC and the ICJ in favor of an objective application of CPWs[116] should also lead to the understanding that a mere apprehension of distress does not suffice in most cases. In this light, expanding 'situation of distress' in Article 24 beyond a real threat to life to include situations of general anxiety or apprehensions of peril, however extreme, could be at odds with the State practice.[117] Secondly, the ILC states that, in order for a plea of distress to be justified, the interests that the State agent seeks to protect must 'clearly outweigh' the other interests at stake.[118] In the same vein, Article 24 (2) (*b*) of the ILC Articles provides that the act must not create a comparable or greater peril. The author believes that the gravity of killing an innocent person not only outweighs the need to validate an erroneous apprehension of danger, but the two situations are manifestly out of balance.

When the case does not involve the use of lethal force by the State agent (or a similarly grave charge), a more lenient rule may be justified. The reason for this variation in treatment is precisely that the CPW of distress is intended to enable the protection of the right to life. If the violation committed by the State agent produces more moderate or reversible consequences, there may be an argument in favor of declaring that 'putative distress' is an acceptable CPW, so long as the interest of safeguarding the right to life is preponderant. The cases involving straying aircraft under unfavorable weather conditions could point in this direction. The apparent threat to life caused by the distress outweighs the moral injury caused by an unauthorized but otherwise harmless overflight or landing, absent other aggravating circumstances. This is shown by the fact that, in the State practice involving such aerial intruders, the sincerity of the pilot's belief that the aircraft's integrity was in danger is rarely called into question or examined too scrupulously. Here there may be a margin of appreciation favoring the person that faces the apparently life-threatening situation, especially when the perception of danger cannot be dispelled at the time of the conduct. In the author's view, this would open the door for a limited form of the theory of mistake of fact, and this would hold so long as the interests protected by the rule that was violated do not outweigh validating the putative threat, and the mistake of fact is objectively reasonable.

---

115 ILC (2001), Art. 24, paras. 2–10.

116 See Sect. 4.2.

117 ILC (2001), Art. 24, paras. 3, 4, 6–8.

118 Ibid., para. 10.

4.4.7 *Case Studies*

(a) **Aerial intrusions**

In exemplifying Article 23's applicability to mistakes, the commentary to the ILC Articles focuses almost exclusively on instances of State aircraft flying into foreign airspace due to weather conditions or failure of navigational equipment.[119] Some of these cases, as well as incidents outlined in the United Nations Secretariat's survey of force majeure and fortuitous events will be discussed in this section.

The first case that will be analyzed dates to 3 April 1913, when a German zeppelin landed in France, carrying five soldiers and seven civilians. The landing was attributed by the zeppelin's crew to weather conditions and equipment malfunction, since the zeppelin's propellers were not working, and the craft had lost its way due to fog. France conducted an official inquiry into the affair, but it allowed the zeppelin to leave the next day without further incident. In response, the German Ambassador to France characterized the French response as 'satisfactory'.[120] France's treatment of the strayed zeppelin, as reported by the United Nations Secretariat,[121] indicates that France did not consider the airspace violation as triggering Germany's responsibility under international law. This is confirmed by a further aerial incident involving France and Germany, just 19 days later, when a German aircraft landed outside Arracourt, France, claiming the same justification as the zeppelin. The United Nations Secretariat notes that

> The [pilots'] explanations appeared to be sufficient to the French civil and military authorities. Towards the evening of the same day, in accordance with instructions received from Paris, the local authorities permitted the pilots to leave . . .[122]

The second case that can be discussed consists in a series of intrusions by German aircraft into Dutch airspace in the context of the First World War.[123] These cases highlight the requirement under customary international law that the mistake of fact be unavoidable and reasonable to excuse the wrongdoing State's responsibility. On 13 April 1915, a German aircraft involved in a training flight landed on the Netherlands due to an error in direction. The Netherlands, which was a neutral State, interned the aircraft and its pilot and refused to release them after repeated requests by Germany. To justify this decision, the Netherlands highlighted the special characteristics of aircraft, including their ease to move and escape control by the territorial State. Although the Netherlands did not charge Germany with any violation of international law, it warned that any plane found flying over its territory would be shot down, and that any aviator that landed on its territory would be interned along with his craft.

A few months later, on 8 September 1915, two German zeppelins crossed the Netherlands' borders. Despite receiving instructions to land by the Dutch authorities,

---

[119] ILC (2001), Art. 23, para. 5.

[120] ILC (1978), pp. 102–103, para. 141.

[121] Ibid.

[122] Ibid., pp. 102–103, para. 142.

[123] ILC (1978), pp. 124–125, paras. 250–254.

the zeppelins refused to do so and continued their way. The Netherlands protested to Germany that, if the zeppelins had mistakenly entered into its airspace due to weather conditions, their conduct would be excusable; what was not excusable was their behavior after learning of their mistake. Germany regretted the incident.[124]

On 1 February 1916, a further German zeppelin flew over the Netherlands. Germany later alleged that the craft had done so due to force majeure; however, the zeppelin never communicated that to the Netherlands. In response to the violation of its airspace, the Netherlands fired upon the zeppelin, which was lost at sea. On 17 February 1916, Germany lamented that the Netherlands had shot at the zeppelin without warning.

The Netherlands replied by characterizing the overflight of German airships as 'acts incompatible with respect for the sovereignty and neutrality of the Netherlands' and noted that 'the most effective means' to avoid such lamentable situations would be for the German aviators to 'keep themselves always far enough away from the maritime and land frontiers of the Netherlands to avoid the possibility of being brought above the territory of the Kingdom either by error or under the influence of atmospheric conditions.'[125] With the repeated instances of mistaken overflight, the publicity of the Netherlands' status as a neutral State and its repeated warnings that aircraft would be brought down, it was up for the German aircraft to exercise due diligence to prevent unauthorized overflight. If aircraft were to fly over the Netherlands' territory, even by mistake caused by weather conditions or malfunction, the airspace violation would be the result of negligence and therefore inexcusable.

This response by the Netherlands does not detract from the idea that, under conditions of mistake (as was the case for the 13 April and 8 September 1915 aerial incidents), the illegality of the overflight could be precluded; it merely highlights that, by the time of the 1 February 1916 incident, such mistakes were already avoidable and even pretextual. This is confirmed by two incidents occurring in 1917, one in May and the other in August, when German planes dropped bombs on the Netherlands supposedly by mistake. Germany justified the bombings by saying that the pilots had gone astray in the clouds; the Netherlands protested the bombings and did not accept the explanation.

The third case under study occurred on 26 April 1917, when a French aircraft bombarded Porrentruy, Switzerland, allegedly by mistake. Expressing regret for the accident, France paid an indemnity for the damage and vowed to investigate and punish the pilot.[126] It is relevant that Porrentruy lies close to the French-Swiss international border, making the mistake plausible.

The preceding cases indicate that violations of airspace by State aircraft are not considered wrongful when they are caused by reasonable and unavoidable mistakes of fact. In contrast, when the mistake was avoidable or there was evidence that it was

[124] Ibid.

[125] Ibid.

[126] ILC (1978), p. 125, para. 256.

pretextual, States did not accept it as a CPW.[127] It is also relevant that in some of these cases, like the 1 February 1916 intrusion by the German zeppelin, analyzed above, express reference was made to force majeure as the legal basis for the justification.

(b) **Innocent passage**

In the context of maritime passage, it is relevant that the doctrine of force majeure is incorporated into treaties on the law of the sea. Each of these provisions, interpreted in light of the applicable international law,[128] would permit the invocation of a mistake of fact. Particularly, Article 18 (2) of the United Nations Convention on the Law of the Sea and Article 14 (3) of the Convention on the Territorial Sea and the Contiguous Zone recognize that the right to innocent passage permits the passing vessel to stop or anchor if such action is necessary due to force majeure. These provisions would be operative, for example, if a vessel stops in the territorial waters of another State, unaware of its location due to weather conditions or failure of its navigational instruments.

4.4.8 Requirements

(a) **'Irresistible force or … unforeseen event': the trigger event**

Under Article 23 of the ILC Articles, the situation of impossibility needs to be caused by an 'irresistible force' or an 'unforeseen event'. These two instances are alternative, as explained previously. The result of this is that Article 23 of the ILC Articles only covers mistakes that are provoked by an external event; it does not cover mistakes that occur spontaneously or due to an internal failure by the State to organize its governmental machinery.

As to the first alternative, the ILC's commentary describes an 'irresistible force' as one that constrains the action of the State, in a way that the State is 'unable to avoid or oppose [it] by its own means'.[129] The character of the force is not relevant; it could either be natural or manmade.[130] What is incorporated into this alternative is the notion of unavoidability: the effects of the impediment must be inevitable for the State. In the context of mistakes of fact, there must be a force that prevents the State from acquiring knowledge that is a physical precondition for its performance; in light of the irresistibility requirement incorporated in Article 23, first alternative,

---

[127] This customary requirement is also showcased by the 1906 shooting of a United States officer by a French warship. The incident was protested by the United States claiming that '[w]hile the killing of Lieutenant England can only be viewed as an accident, it cannot be regarded as belonging to the unavoidable class whereby no responsibility is entailed'. This incident prompted France to provide adequate reparations. ILC (2001), Art. 23 footnote 347.

[128] Article 31 (3) (*c*) of the Vienna Convention on the Law of Treaties.

[129] ILC (2001), Art. 23, para. 2.

[130] Ibid., para. 3.

the State must not be in conditions to dissipate or refute the mistake through its own means, as otherwise the compelling force could not be characterized as 'irresistible'.

In contrast, in the second alternative, the existence of an 'unforeseen event' suffices to trigger Article 23. For the event to be 'unforeseen' for the purposes of Article 23, it suffices that the event was not 'easily foreseeable' for the State. Thus, Article 23 precludes wrongfulness unless the event causing the impossibility could have readily been anticipated and the State failed to take reasonable steps to do so. In the context of mistakes, the State must ensure that its awareness of the circumstances underlying the performance of its obligations is not obscured by an event it could have easily anticipated.

In combination, these two alternatives suggest that the test to examine whether the trigger event can be invoked under Article 23 is twofold: could the occurrence have been easily anticipated by the wrongdoing State? If not, could it have been avoided? The State's invocation of Article 23 will fail if either question can be answered in the affirmative. This is confirmed by the United Nations Secretariat's survey of State practice, which defines force majeure as either an 'unforeseen' event, or one that is 'foreseen but inevitable or irresistible' for the responsible State.[131] This also suggests that unlike in most domestic systems,[132] the force majeure defense under Article 23 does not make unforeseeability a general requirement for all cases, nor does it consider unforeseeability and irresistibility as cumulative requirements.

(b) **'Beyond the control of the State': externality**

Article 23 of the ILC Articles requires the event to be 'beyond the control of the State'; it must be external to that State. This element of Article 23 is not covered by the ILC's commentary; however, its content can be discerned by reference to Article 23 (2), which contains two exceptions to the general rule of force majeure:

> Paragraph 1 does not apply if:
>
> (*a*) the situation of force majeure is due, either alone or in combination with other factors, to the conduct of the State invoking it; or
>
> (*b*) the State has assumed the risk of that situation occurring.

In principle, if the situation of force majeure is attributable to the State, it cannot be deemed to be beyond its control (Article 23 (2) (*a*)). Therefore, Article 23 will not apply if the situation in question falls within any of the forms of attribution recognized under international law. This includes the acts of the State's officials, organs and institutions (Article 4), those of entities exercising elements of governmental authority (Article 5), those of non-State actors under the effective control of the responsible State (Article 8) or whose conduct is acknowledged and adopted by the State (Article 11). Moreover, the concept of externality must be defined by reference to the risk allocation underlying the obligation that was breached. If the State assumed the risk of the situation of force majeure, it cannot then invoke that

[131] ILC (1978), p. 69, para. 13.

[132] Schwenzer et al. (2012), para. 45.33.

situation as a circumstance precluding the wrongfulness of its conduct under Article 23 (paragraph 2 (*b*)). This is particularly relevant when the obligation results from a treaty, where the risks are contractually allocated between the State parties, either expressly or implicitly. According to the ILC, Article 23 (2) (*b*) applies also in cases where the State has 'undertaken to prevent the particular situation arising'.[133] In this sense, Article 23 (2) of the ILC Articles can be seen as a development of the requirement that the situation of force majeure fall outside the State's control under paragraph 1.

Applied to the theory of mistake, Article 23 of the ILC Articles will not be operative if the mistake in question derives from the State's own governmental machinery or if the State assumed the risk of the error. Reference can be made to the ICJ's decision in the *Temple of Preah Vihear* case, where the Court found that Thailand's alleged error had been a risk assumed by Thailand judging by the way the relevant instruments had been drawn up.[134] Article 23 (1) applies even when the State has contributed to the situation of force majeure by error or without knowing it, even if the mistake was made in good faith.[135]

(c) 'Materially Impossible'

Article 23 requires the external event in question to make performance of the obligation 'materially impossible' for the State. This means that the State must not have a real possibility of escaping the effects of the impediment to performance.[136]

Therefore, in principle, the performance of the obligation must be objectively impossible. However, with the rapid increase of technical and technological capabilities, the scope of what is objectively impossible has been reduced significantly. Endeavors that in the past were actually impossible are now possible with some degree of onerousness. Consider, as some authors have suggested, the recovery of a ship that has sunk to the bottom of a body of water.[137] The increase in the capability of society to achieve what was previously impossible has made it legally necessary to redefine the concept of impossibility. Some authors have suggested that these developments have blurred the line between impossibility (associated with force majeure) and excessive onerousness (associated with the *théorie de l'imprévision*, hardship and similar doctrines).[138] The commentary to the ILC Articles, however, appears to reject this view, indicating that excessive onerousness is not contemplated by the Articles as part of the concept of force majeure.[139] This view appears to conflict with the ICJ's Judgment in the *Gabčíkovo-Nagymaros Project* case, where the Court pointed out that the impossibility of paying a debt out of 'serious financial difficulties' could lead to the preclusion of responsibility for the breach of a treaty, despite

---

[133] ILC (2001), Art. 23, para. 10.

[134] ICJ (1962), p. 25.

[135] Hentrei and Soley (2011), para. 15.

[136] ILC (2001), Art. 23, para. 3.

[137] Ishida (2018), pp. 364–368.

[138] Brunner (2019), para. 27.

[139] ILC (2001), Art. 23, para. 3.

the fact that it would not trigger the suspension of that treaty under Article 61 of the Vienna Convention on the Law of Treaties.[140]

In the context of the mistake of fact theory, Article 23 will preclude the wrongfulness of conduct in cases where the accurate appreciation of a fact was a physical precondition for the performance of the obligation. This must be analyzed on a case-by-case basis ('in the circumstances').

4.5 Putative Necessity

The notion of 'putative necessity' covers the situation in which a State acts believing, wrongly, that its actions are 'the only way … to safeguard an essential interest against a grave and imminent peril', as codified in Article 25 of the ILC's Articles on State Responsibility.

The general rule for CPWs that responsibility remains objective[141] also appears to operate in this area, as shown by the ICJ's *Gabčíkovo-Nagymaros Project* Judgment. In that case, the Court affirmed that necessity was a CPW and that its manifestation in the Articles on State Responsibility (Article 25 in the present codification; Article 33 in the Articles as drafted at the time of the Court's decision) reflected customary international law,[142] including the different conditions laid down in the relevant provision.[143] The Court was faced with this institution of international law due to an argument raised by Hungary to justify the suspension of its obligations under the 1977 Treaty concerning the construction and operation of the Gabčíkovo-Nagymaros System of Locks. Particularly, Hungary relied on an 'ecological state of necessity', citing doubts as to how putting the project into operation might affect the natural environment, a question which according to Hungary required new scientific studies on the matter.

The ICJ highlighted that it, too, placed great importance in the protection of the environment, which it considered to have passed into the corpus of international law.[144] However, the Court did not consider that the 'uncertainties'[145] cited by Hungary were enough to open the door for the invocation of necessity:

> The Court considers, however, that, serious though these uncertainties might have been they could not, alone, establish the *objective existence of a "peril" in the sense of a component element of a state of necessity*. The word "peril" certainly evokes the idea of "risk"; that is precisely what distinguishes "peril" from material damage. But *a state of necessity could*

[140] ICJ (1997), para. 102. On the other hand, note the ICJ's finding in *Belgium* v. *Senegal* that 'the financial difficulties raised by Senegal cannot justify the fact that it failed to initiate proceedings against Mr. Habré.' ICJ (2012), para. 112.

[141] See Sect. 4.2.

[142] ICJ (1997), paras. 50, 51.

[143] Ibid., para. 52.

[144] Ibid., para. 53.

[145] Ibid., para. 54.

> *not exist without a "peril" duly established at the relevant point in time; the mere apprehension of a possible "peril" could not suffice in that respect.* It could moreover hardly be otherwise, when the "peril" constituting the state of necessity has at the time to be "grave" and "imminent". *"Imminence" is synonymous with "immediacy" or "proximity" and goes far beyond the concept of "possibility".* As the International Law Commission emphasized in its commentary, the "extremely grave and imminent" peril must "have been a threat to the interest at the actual time" ...
>
> The Hungarian argument on the state of necessity could not convince the Court unless it was at least proven that a *real*, "grave" and "imminent" "peril" existed in 1989 and that the measures taken by Hungary were the only possible response to it...[146]

Some significant elements of this explanation are worth mentioning here. The first is that the Court inferred the objective standard to be applied to the existence of a 'peril' under the necessity provision of the ILC's Articles from context. It ascribed particular importance to the fact that the peril had to be 'imminent', which in its view presupposed (future and immediate) objective existence. It also distinguished between a 'risk' of environmental harm from actual 'material damage', which not only influence the *ratione temporis* elements of the definition of necessity (that the State's conduct is, theoretically, being applied before the risk materializes) but also confirms that the threat posed to the State's interest had to be an objective probability. Thus, Hungary had to establish a 'real' threat, not merely uncertainties about the dangers of the project. The ICJ's conclusion that, without delving into the question of gravity, the perils invoked by Hungary 'were not sufficiently established in 1989, nor were they "imminent"'[147] confirms that the existence of the peril and its imminence and gravity are separate requirements under Article 25 of the Articles on State Responsibility. Taken together, these statements by the Court confirm that the standard to be applied to the CPW of necessity is an objective one.

The ILC appears to share this view. Indeed, it has pointed out that '[t]he peril has to be objectively established and not merely apprehended as possible'.[148] It is important to note that although it conceives that a peril that is 'merely apprehended or contingent' is 'not sufficient',[149] the ILC is not of the view that absolute certainty is required in all cases. In some instances, precautionary action may be taken. If 'the peril is clearly established on the basis of the evidence reasonably available at the time', the State may decide to proceed despite there being a 'measure of uncertainty'.[150] This is especially true in the environmental realm, where there may be 'issues of scientific uncertainty and different views ... taken by informed experts' as to the existence, gravity or imminence of the peril.[151]

The author believes that this does not mean that a mistake of fact may be accepted in the context of necessity. Indeed, in many cases the State may need to act on a precautionary basis to prevent a grave danger from materializing, as this falls

---

[146] Ibid. (emphasis added).

[147] Ibid., para. 57.

[148] ILC (2001), Art. 25, para. 15.

[149] Ibid., para. 16.

[150] Ibid.

[151] Ibid.

within the concept of necessity by definition.[152] The objectivity of international responsibility is not intended to cause a regulatory freeze in these cases. However, if the State turns out to be wrong or to have acted based on a faulty determination, it needs to bear the injurious consequences that follow. In the end, unless the applicable law provides otherwise, uncertainty and urgency are not a *carte blanche* to avoid making reparation for a duly established harm. When acting preemptively, the State assumes the risk of making an incorrect assessment. The author believes that this approach is justified. Indeed, the purpose of the defense of necessity is to cover only the gravest threats to a State's sovereign interests, justifying an extreme course of action.[153] Accepting 'putative necessity' risks diluting the regime of international responsibility and undermining the principle of *pacta sunt servanda.*

4.6 Putative Self-defense

4.6.1 Introduction

The legal basis for self-defense in the post-Second World War international order is Article 51 of the United Nations Charter, which largely codifies customary international law.[154] It reads as follows:

> Nothing in the present Charter shall impair the inherent right of individual or collective self-defence if an armed attack occurs against a Member of the United Nations, until the Security Council has taken measures necessary to maintain international peace and security. Measures taken by Members in the exercise of this right of self-defence shall be immediately reported to the Security Council and shall not in any way affect the authority and responsibility of the Security Council under the present Charter to take at any time such action as it deems necessary in order to maintain or restore international peace and security.

Self-defense is one of the two undisputedly recognized exceptions to the prohibition on the use of force found in Article 2 (4) of the United Nations Charter, which in turn is a codification of a peremptory norm of general international law (*jus cogens*), from which no derogation is permitted under any circumstances.[155] The other recognized exception is, of course, the application of enforcement measures by the United Nations Security Council acting under the authority of Chapter VII of the Charter, when faced with a threat to international peace, a breach of the peace or an act of aggression.[156] These two exceptions are part of a larger whole that constitutes the United Nations Collective Security System, the aim of which is to set out normative, political and military conditions for the resort to force in circumstances where it is

[152] Ibid.

[153] Ibid., paras. 14–16.

[154] ICJ (1986), para. 176.

[155] ILC (2022), Annex (a).

[156] See Article 39 of the United Nations Charter. This book will not delve into the question whether other justifications for the use of force are permitted under international law.

needed to prevent and address threats to international peace and security. Indeed, as was pointed out before, self-defense is regulated as a purely temporary institution, allowed as a mechanism to protect a State's political independence or territorial integrity against foreign armed aggression, pending a decision on the matter by the United Nations Security Council. It follows that unilateral forceful action is subject to strict prerequisites and conditions imposed by international law, to prevent the cure from transforming into the malady.

At the same time, the situations calling for the exercise of defensive unilateral force by a State, like other circumstances addressed in this book, often require quick decision-making and reaction to prevent an armed aggression from causing catastrophic injury. In this process, mistakes can be made, also often with disastrous consequences. At the center of the interplay between the consequences of idleness, on the one hand, and hasty reaction, on the other, lies the question of mistakes of fact, standing shoulder-to-shoulder with other theoretical problems that plague the discussion of what the legal prerequisites are to resort to the use of force without violating Article 2 (4) of the Charter. The theory of mistake of fact was, however, one of the problems that received the least attention in the legal literature, although academic awareness of it has increased in recent years. One of the most significant treatments of this question was put forward by Marko Milanovic in a three-part analysis posted on the blog of the European Journal of International Law (EJIL:Talk!) in January 2020 following the shootdown of Ukraine International Airlines Flight PS752.[157] This sparked some interest in academic circles.[158] In his analysis of the *jus ad bellum*, Milanovic pointed out that this question could not be resolved simply by looking at the language of Article 51 of the United Nations Charter alone, although some parts of it[159] might point to an objective standard of responsibility. Milanovic's conclusion leaned in favor of applying an objective standard to Article 51 of the Charter, noting that although some latitude could arguably be given in cases of on-the-spot defensive measures, he could not see why in such cases the injured State would not be entitled to reparation.[160]

4.6.2 Mistake of Fact and the Prohibition of the Use of Force

The focus of this general section, as its title indicates, is the inherent right to self-defense under Article 51 of the United Nations Charter. Conversely, the author does not address in length the prohibition of the use of force under Article 2 (4). However, the relationship between the two provisions does call for some clarification. Article 2 (4) reads as follows:

---

[157] Milanovic (2020a, b, c); see also Chap. 3, Sect. 3.2.1.

[158] Sukumar (2021), Lahmann (2020).

[159] Particularly, the language 'if an armed attack occurs', which will be analyzed later in this section.

[160] Milanovic (2020b).

> All Members shall refrain in their international relations from the threat or use of force against the territorial integrity or political independence of any State, or in any other manner inconsistent with the Purposes of the United Nations.

This prohibition is clear, unequivocal and categorical. It declares illegal the resort to the threat or use of force against another State as a tool of foreign policy. As mentioned before, this prohibition reflects a norm of the highest order in the international system: it is a norm of *jus cogens*, from which no derogation is permitted. Indeed, this norm has been described as the cornerstone of the modern international legal system.[161] The exceptions to this rule are few and far between. It is clear that the theory of mistake of fact has not gained enough acceptance in the practice of States to arrive at the conclusion that it has somehow passed into the corpus of *jus cogens*, so as to challenge the scope of the prohibition of the use of force. Moreover, given the absence of a mental requirement in the primary rule of Article 2 (4), a mistake of fact could not prevent a finding that a particular forceful action qualifies as a prohibited use of force triggering international responsibility.

The ample scope of this prohibition confirms that it cannot be curtailed by such a doctrine. The ordinary language of Article 2 (4) covers all uses of force, whatever their scale, nature or gravity, unless they fall under one of the grounds of exception. In that sense, it is worth noting the final clause of Article 2 (4) of the Charter, which specifies that States shall refrain from using or threatening 'force against the territorial integrity or political independence of any State, or in any other manner inconsistent with the Purposes of the United Nations'. This should not lead the interpreter to the conclusion that some uses of force that are somehow viewed as 'consistent with the Purposes of the United Nations' should be permitted. This clause does not seek to enlarge or diminish the scope of the prohibition of the use of force, but merely to clarify that any use of force not otherwise exonerated by the Charter is, indeed, incompatible with the United Nations' aims.

Article 2 (4) codifies a general ban encompassing *all* manifestations of the use of force, regardless of the motivation behind them (save for those exceptionally permitted), and not only those that are expressly mentioned in that final clause. As Ruys explains, Article 2 (4) of the United Nations Charter expanded the scope of the prohibition under the Kellogg-Briand Pact of 1928, which outlawed war, to proscribe even small-scale uses of force and threats of force.[162] In effect, the final clause of Article 2 (4) was drafted to ensure that the ban on the use of force would be comprehensive and all-inclusive. During the United Nations Conference on International Organization, while considering the text of what would later become Article 2 (4), delegations expressed some concerns that the formulation could lead to the interpretation that some uses of force outside those regulated in the Charter would be permissible. The Brazilian delegate, for example, pointed to the ambiguity of the text and complained that 'the text as it stood at present might well be interpreted as authorizing the use of force unilaterally by a State, claiming that such action

[161] Randelzhofer and Dörr (2012), p. 203, Tladi (2022), pp. 46–47, Gray (2008), p. 31.

[162] Ruys (2010), p. 55.

was in accordance with the purposes of the Organization'.[163] The Belgian delegate replied that the language 'in any other manner' was intended to prevent this.[164] The Norwegian delegate said that 'it should be made very clear in the Report to the Commission that [Article 2 (4)] did not contemplate any use of force, outside of action by the Organization, going beyond individual or collective self-defense'.[165] The United States delegate confirmed that 'the intention of the authors of the original text was to state in the broadest terms an absolute all-inclusive prohibition' and that 'the phrase "or in any other manner" was designed to insure that there should be no loopholes'.[166] Tladi, for instance, interprets that this final phrase is a clarification that any extraterritorial use of force without consent would violate the territorial integrity and political independence of the State.[167]

Hence, a doctrine of mistake of fact, whatever its content, could be construed as an example of the kind of loophole that the final clause of Article 2 (4) was intended to close. This is why the present inquiry focuses on whether so-called 'putative' self-defense is admissible under international law in accordance with Article 51 of the Charter; indeed, this is the only aspect of the prohibition of the use of force where the theory of mistake of fact could, in principle, have any impact.

In that respect, the prohibition under Article 2 (4) is broader in scope than the right to self-defense in Article 51. In other words, States are not entitled to resort to defensive force in response to any and every attack or incident. Article 51 circumscribes this right to situations where a Member of the United Nations has become the victim of an 'armed attack'. The Court acknowledged this difference in scope of application in *Nicaragua*, firstly, when it noted that an 'armed attack' encompasses the 'most grave forms of the use of force'[168]; secondly, when it distinguished between an 'armed attack' and a 'mere frontier incident'[169]; and thirdly, when it declared, in the context of collective self-defense, that there is no such right in respect of a use of force that falls short of the threshold of 'armed attack'.[170] The fact that Article 2 (4) has a wider scope than Article 51 of the United Nations Charter is also suggested by the reference to *threats* of force, which are not encompassed by the express terms of Article 51. The incomplete overlap between Articles 2 (4) and 51 of the Charter means that a large category of uses of force, not eligible for self-defense for various reasons, is also not eligible for consideration under the theory of mistake of fact. Without delving yet into the effect of a mistake of fact on a self-defense plea, the author concludes that such uses of force that fall outside Article 51 of the United Nations Charter would be illegal even if committed under the influence of a mistake

[163] UNCIO 1945 VI, p. 334.

[164] Ibid.

[165] Ibid.

[166] Ibid., p. 335.

[167] Tladi (2022), pp. 47–48 (emphasis added).

[168] ICJ (1986), para. 191.

[169] Ibid., para. 195.

[170] Ibid., para. 211.

of fact. To hold otherwise would do violence to the language of Article 2 (4) of the Charter and significantly weaken the prohibition.

4.6.3 'If an Armed Attack Occurs': Imaginary Attacks and Anticipatory Self-defense

The archetypical case of mistake of fact in the context of Article 51, and indeed the inciting example for this book,[171] is the case where a State responds with armed force to a perceived threat that is later found to have been non-existent. Throughout this book, examples have been given for attacks on civilian aircraft under the incorrect belief that they constituted a military threat.[172] These cases are especially challenging because a full answer cannot be derived from the blackletter of Article 51 of the Charter. Although what stands to the eye of the interpreter is the fact that Article 51 of the Charter requires the actual occurrence of an armed attack to trigger the right to self-defense ('…if an armed attack *occurs*…', '… dans le cas où un Membre des Nations Unies *est* l'objet d'une agression armée…'[173]), this has not prevented scholars and governments from claiming a right to self-defense when it is required *before* this temporal threshold has been crossed, i.e. the so-called anticipatory self-defense doctrine.

In the scarce academic literature that exists to tackle the question of mistake of fact in this context, sometimes a connection between putative and anticipatory self-defense is identified[174] but later discarded.[175] Indeed, it is undeniable that these two doctrines address different situations. While *anticipatory self-defense* concerns the right of a State to resort to defensive force against a future but imminent attack, *putative self-defense* concerns the possibility of resorting to force when the State *believes* that an imminent attack will materialize, and this belief turns out to be incorrect. In the first case, the attack has not occurred *yet*; in the second, the attack was *never* going to occur. Legally and theoretically, academics are right to exercise caution to avoid conflating these two concepts. The problem is that, in practice, the distinction between the two scenarios can blur away. The State that resorts to force anticipating an attack will insist on its imminence, perhaps even claiming that the non-occurrence of the attack is precisely due to the armed intervention. On the other hand, the State victim of the allegedly defensive force will likely insist on the attack's factual non-existence or improbability. In other words, the first State is likely to view this constellation of cases as examples of anticipatory self-defense, while the second State would probably rely on the impermissibility of a doctrine of putative self-defense, even if in either case the argumentation of these propositions is not explicit. The

---

[171] See Chap. 1.

[172] See Chap. 3, Sect. 3.2.1.

[173] Emphasis added.

[174] De Luca (2012), pp. 52–52.

[175] E.g., Sukumar (2021).

reason for this conundrum is that these two scenarios can be indistinguishable if one looks only at the factual indicia used by the defending State when deciding whether to use force. The difference can often only be discerned in hindsight, when the alleged attack is proven to have been either imminent or imaginary. The conclusion that the author draws from this is that the factual connection that may exist between anticipatory and putative self-defense should not be discarded too quickly. The State practice and legal literature on anticipatory self-defense may well provide some insight as to how the question of putative self-defense is to be resolved.

The debate as to the permissibility of anticipatory self-defense has been aptly described as a 'never-ending saga'.[176] Although the answer to this doctrinal debate lies outside the scope of this book, it is worth pointing out that the attitudes adopted by States when justifying the use of force are essential in understanding how to deal with putative self-defense. This debate as to the allowable forms of self-defense (be it strictly reactive, interceptive, preemptive or preventive[177]) is significant because it proves that, at some level, the consensus among States is that, at the very least, an armed attack needs to exist as an actual fact, or its imminence needs to be factually demonstrable. Rather than challenging this, the discourse on anticipatory self-defense focuses on determining what the *required degree of imminence* is to trigger Article 51 of the United Nations Charter. In line with what the ICJ stated in *Nicaragua*,[178] the significance of this attitude is to confirm rather than deny that a real armed attack remains a *sine qua non* requirement for invoking self-defense.

At the same, to rely too much on the factual similarity of cases of anticipatory and putative self-defense would be admittedly fallacious. Although States may be reacting to the same indicia to resort to unilateral force, the legal difference between a future and an imaginary attack is too large. After surveying the academic positions on the question of anticipatory self-defense, Ruys observes that the post-9/11 consensus appears to be that licit self-defense under Article 51 lies somewhere between *preemptive* self-defense, which responds to an imminent attack, and *interceptive* self-defense, which responds to an attack that has been launched but has not struck the victim State (see Fig. 4.1).[179]

Where does putative self-defense lie in this spectrum? In truth, given the non-existence of an armed attack in these constellations, putative self-defense should not even fall within this spectrum at all. However, if the theoretical exercise were to be entertained, it certainly could not fall within the pole of 'reactive' self-defense, since an armed attack has not occurred nor is it ongoing. Within the pole of 'anticipatory' self-defense, putative self-defense would be closer to the position of *preventive* self-defense (i.e. allegedly defensive force that responds to a non-imminent threat to

---

[176] Ruys (2010), p. 255.

[177] This classification is based on Ruys' analysis of this question. See Ruys (2010), pp. 253–254.

[178] ICJ (1986), para. 186.

[179] Ruys (2010), pp. 264–267.

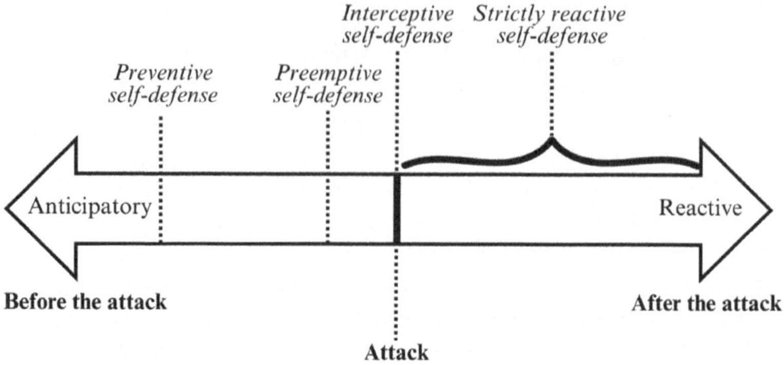

Fig. 4.1 This diagram, based on Ruys' analysis of the different doctrines of self-defense,[180] illustrates the temporal spectrum of defensive force in individual cases

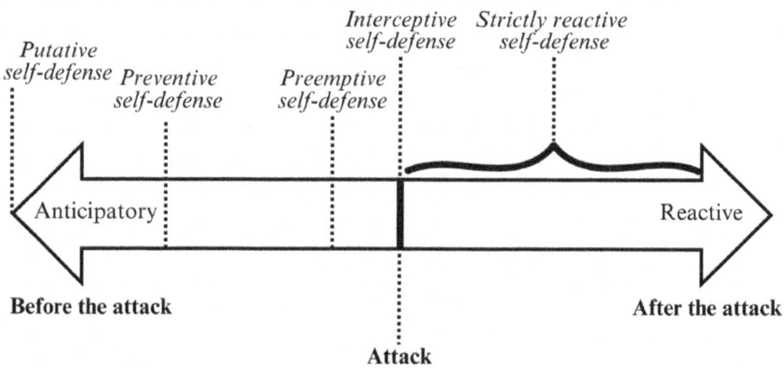

Fig. 4.2 Theoretical positioning of putative self-defense in Ruys' terminological classification

national security, in an attempt to prevent it from becoming imminent[181]), if only closer to the left side of the spectrum, as a more extreme manifestation of anticipatory self-defense (see Fig. 4.2). Here the threat not only has no concrete manifestations—but it is also non-existent. Considering that the consensus leans in favor of rejecting preventive self-defense as a permissible exception to the use of force prohibition,[182] it stands to reason that putative self-defense should be unacceptable *a fortiori.*

In other words, whatever one's views are as to whether the term 'occurs' in Article 51 can be interpreted to mean 'is about to occur' or 'will occur imminently', it is undeniable that the chasm one needs to cross to interpret it as 'was believed to be about to occur' is vastly greater. The author believes that it defies the permissible parameters of interpretation. It contradicts the very logic of self-defense and blurs the line that separates it from aggression. It stretches the prohibition on the use of

[180] Ibid., p. 254

[181] Ibid.

[182] Ibid., p. 264.

force far beyond its breaking point. It turns the strict requirements of self-defense into an exercise of divining subjective perception. Crucially, it obliterates Article 2 (4)'s *effet utile*.

The better position, and in the author's view the only position that prevents unnecessary escalation and international violence, is that so-called putative self-defense is in reality an aggressive use of force prohibited by international law, however understandable the factual circumstances that might have led to it.

Of course, international law may not have at present the capacity to stay the hand of a government that genuinely (but incorrectly) believes that its population or territory is under imminent military threat. The question is rather who should assume the risk of the mistake: the State who made it, or the State who innocently suffered its consequences despite not having breached the prohibition of the use of force. The author's view is that rejecting a theory of putative self-defense is the best way of apportioning this risk. This is consistent with the standard of objective State responsibility adopted by the ILC in its Articles on the subject.[183] Indeed, as transpires with any other CPW,[184] a State that resorts to self-defense based on its unilateral assessment of the situation 'does so at its own risk and may incur responsibility for its own wrongful conduct in the event of an incorrect assessment'.[185] Excluding a mere perception of an armed attack from the remit of Article 51 of the Charter also mirrors the ICJ's treatment of necessity in the *Gabčíkovo-Nagymaros Project* case, where imminence was interpreted as presupposing real existence.[186]

Perhaps an example showing the impermissibility of putative self-defense is provided by the ongoing war of aggression waged by the Russian Federation against Ukraine since 24 February 2022. Though the Russian Federation's excuses for the military invasion have varied over time, one of the key claims by Russia[187] was based on Ukraine's decision to strengthen its bonds with the West and its desire to join the European Union and the North Atlantic Treaty Organization (NATO). Russia has accused NATO of building military capabilities in Ukraine in anticipation for an imminent aggression against Russia,[188] which it considered as sufficient reason to invoke Article 51 of the United Nations Charter.[189] The reaction of a significant portion of the international community has been overwhelmingly to reject this narrative as untrue, deploring the 'special military operation' as an illegal, 'unprovoked'[190]

---

[183] See Chap. 3, Sect. 3.1.

[184] Article 21 of the Articles on State Responsibility.

[185] ILC (2001), Art. 49, para. 3.

[186] See Sect. 4.2.

[187] Other claims included unsubstantiated allegations of genocide by the Ukrainian Government against populations residing in Eastern Ukraine, especially the Donetsk and Lugansk oblasts. This forced Ukraine to bring an ICJ claim against Russia positing that this attitude, and the ensuing use of force, violated the spirit of the Genocide Convention. See ICJ (2022), para. 59.

[188] Welle (2023).

[189] ICJ (2022), paras. 32, 33, 39.

[190] European Union (2022), United States (2022a), Czech Republic (2022), Guatemala and Ukraine (2022), Antigua and Barbuda et al. (2022), United Nations (2022b).

act of aggression in violation of Charter Article 2 (4).[191] The author believes that the attitude to treat this situation as an unprovoked aggression, despite Russia's claims of self-defense, shows that putative self-defense is not acceptable in international law. It confirms that the objective existence of an armed attack is a *sine qua non* requirement for Article 51.

The one authority that is sometimes used to justify the existence of a limited doctrine of putative self-defense is the USS *Vincennes* incident, briefly addressed in a previous chapter.[192] As explained before, in this case a United States navy cruiser shot down an Iranian civil aircraft under the mistaken belief that it was a military plane about to launch an attack on the warship. On a letter dated 6 July 1988,[193] three days after the incident, the United States reported to the United Nations Security Council, in accordance with Article 51 of the Charter, that '[i]n the course of the United States response to [an attack by small Iranian boats], the *Vincennes* fired in self-defense at what it believed to be a hostile Iranian military aircraft, after sending repeated warnings (to which the aircraft did not respond).'[194] The United States maintained that, although it deeply regretted the tragic loss of life resulting from the attack, the USS *Vincennes* had acted lawfully under Article 51 of the United Nations Charter.[195]

The possibility of invoking self-defense to justify the use of weapons against a civil aircraft in flight is contemplated in Article 3 *bis* (*a*) of the Chicago Convention on International Civil Aviation, which reflects customary international law.[196] Indeed, Article 3 *bis* (*a*) provides that

> The contracting States recognize that every State must refrain from resorting to the use of weapons against civil aircraft in flight and that, in case of interception, the lives of persons on board and the safety of aircraft must not be endangered. *This provision shall not be interpretated as modifying in any way the rights and obligations of States set forth in the Charter of the United Nations.*[197]

This passage is widely understood to refer to the right to self-defense under Article 51 of the Charter.[198] The drafting history of Article 3 *bis* shows that preference was expressed for a general reference to the Charter, without specific mention of Article 51, due to the fear that such a mention would be misconstrued as an authorization to use force against civilian planes.[199] Yet, the attitude of the negotiating States was overwhelmingly to consider Article 51 as 'the only legitimate exception justifying the use of force against civil aircraft'.[200]

---

[191] UN Doc A/RES/ES-11/1 operative, para. 2.

[192] See Chap. 3, Sect. 3.2.1.

[193] It is worth noting that Iran also sent a letter to the Security Council on 5 July 1988. See UN Doc S/19981.

[194] UN Doc S/19989 (italics in the original).

[195] Ibid.

[196] Geiß (2005), p. 228.

[197] Emphasis added.

[198] Geiß (2005), p. 237.

[199] Ibid., p. 245.

[200] Ibid.

At the ensuing Security Council meeting, the United States delegation offered *ex gratia* compensation for the victims of the USS *Vincennes* incident, as a 'prompt reaction from a President and a country that ... feel compassion for those who innocently lost their lives' and, at the same time, 'strictly as a humanitarian gesture, not as a matter of legal obligation, but out of a sense of moral compassion, reflecting the value that we place on human life.'[201] From this meeting emerged Security Council resolution 616 (1988), which deplored the tragic loss of life of the victims but did not assign legal responsibility to the United States.

Security Council resolution 616 (1988), however, only paints a fraction of the picture. The author believes that the answer as to the value of this precedent as evidence of the existence of the doctrine of putative self-defense lies in the discussions leading to this resolution. During the fateful Security Council meeting, several participating States made statements on the incident. Most of the statements that addressed the incident from a legal perspective condemned the action as a violation of international law. The Soviet Union questioned 'how can one regard as self-defense the destruction of a passenger airliner flying within an established air corridor'.[202] Nepal expressed a preference for an unqualified admission of responsibility by the United States and the granting of full reparation to Iran and the families of the victims.[203] The People's Republic of China expressed itself in similar lines.[204] The United Arab Emirates declared that the United States bore 'full responsibility for the tragedy' and faulted it for not ensuring that its attack was being directed against a military target.[205] Syria called it a violation of human rights.[206] Libya went further and called it a 'barbaric act of aggression'.[207] Yugoslavia branded it an 'irresponsible and incomprehensible act', which was 'in contravention of international law'.[208]

The States that did not condemn the shootdown as a violation of international law, like the United Kingdom,[209] Italy,[210] France,[211] Argentina,[212] Japan,[213] Germany,[214]

[201] UN Doc S/PV.2818, 58.

[202] UN Doc S/PV.2819, p. 18.

[203] Ibid., p. 8.

[204] Ibid., pp. 29–30.

[205] Ibid., p. 55.

[206] UN Doc S/PV.2820, p. 21.

[207] Ibid., p. 16.

[208] UN Doc S/PV.2819, pp. 14–15.

[209] Ibid., pp. 5–7.

[210] Ibid., pp. 21–25.

[211] Ibid., pp. 26–28.

[212] Ibid., p. 33.

[213] Ibid., pp. 39–40.

[214] Ibid., pp. 43–45.

Senegal,[215] Zambia,[216] Pakistan,[217] India,[218] and Brazil,[219] expressed deep regret for the incident and welcomed the United States offer of *ex gratia* compensation for the families of the victims, but did not expressly delve into any legal aspects of the incident.[220] These discussions show great division which, politically motivated or not, denies them the status of subsequent practice.[221] Moreover, it should not be forgotten that the relevance of Security Council resolutions for proving general practice of States is limited.[222] It is notable that most of the States that made statements based on international law declared that a violation of it had occurred, and those who seemed to adopt a contrary view used political language instead. Furthermore, the lack of condemnation for the shootdown in resolution 616 likely was a compromise reached to prevent a United States veto rather than evidence of a consensus grounded in international law. The author believes that the USS *Vincennes* incident does not confirm any doctrine of putative self-defense that could change the interpretation of Charter Article 51.

Subsequent practice, in fact, would appear to point in the opposite direction. Other incidents involving the mistaken use of armed force against civil aircraft in flight, already addressed in previous chapters,[223] also led to States complaining of numerous violations of international law. This fact is at variance with the assertion that the wrongfulness of such actions could have been precluded on the basis of some form of putative self-defense. In the author's view, these cases, taken as a whole, prove that putative self-defense is not a cognizable rule of international law. The unavoidable consequence is that a mistake of fact as to the *existence* of an armed attack against the State invoking Article 51 undermines the plea of self-defense, potentially transforming any ensuing use of force based on the perceived attack into an act of aggression.

An interesting point to note is that these cases involving the unintentional use of force against the State adopting defensive measures[224] could fit into this category as well. Indeed, if a use of force without *animus aggressionis* is not considered an armed attack, then in both categories of cases the State is not responding to an attack covered by Article 51 of the Charter. If these categories were conflated, the *Oil Platforms* and *Nicaragua* cases could be construed as further indications that putative self-defense is not accepted in international law. While for theoretical reasons the author prefers to maintain the two constellations separate, it is worth pointing out that in both archetypes the mistakes of fact involved (made by the defending State,

---

215 Ibid., p. 47.

216 UN Doc S/PV.2820, p. 8.

217 Ibid., p. 12.

218 Ibid., pp. 23–25.

219 Ibid., p. 38.

220 Milanovic (2020b).

221 ILC (2018), conclusion 4, para. 16.

222 ICJ (2010), para. 81.

223 See Chap. 3, Sect. 3.2.1.

224 See Sect. 4.6.4.

the State responsible for the original incident, or both) militate against the possibility of relying on a plea of self-defense.

4.6.4 *'Against': The Problem of* Animus Aggressionis

The precondition for the right to self-defense to come into operation under Article 51 is the occurrence of an 'armed attack'. A second constellation of cases, perhaps easier to analyze, concerns the example of a State that becomes the victim of the use of armed force committed by another State, who orchestrated the alleged attack by mistake or accident. This category of cases demands analysis of a central question in the international law of the use of force: does the law require a particular state of mind on the part of the State for the resort to force to trigger Article 51 of the United Nations Charter? Does Article 51 require the State behind the alleged 'armed attack' to have had a particular subjective intent or state of mind then resorting to the use of force?

This was a question that arose in the negotiations that led to the adoption of United Nations General Assembly resolution 3314 (XXIX) on the Definition of Aggression.[225] Although analyzing in depth the distinction between aggression and armed attack goes beyond the scope of this chapter, it is worth noting that some of the passages of these negotiations shed light on whether a use of force orchestrated by mistake is to be considered an 'armed attack' for the purposes of United Nations Charter Article 51 or not. In the ILC, Special Rapporteur Spiropoulos expressed the view that 'aggressive intention' was required for the first use of force to constitute an act of aggression.[226] While accepting this general view, some members of the Commission argued that the mere act of using force often was enough evidence of a subjective *animus aggressionis*, especially when used in a manner and for purposes that were 'contrary to the present international order'.[227]

The same juxtaposition surfaced again in the United Nations General Assembly, with a group of States arguing that the controlling criterion should be the subjective goal of the attack, identifying a list of prohibited aims for the use of force based on territorial integrity[228] and political independence[229] (*principle of intent*) and another group positing that the first use of force should automatically be regarded as aggressive (*principle of priority*).[230] It has been pointed out that the principle of priority

---

[225] For a more detailed analysis of this discussion, see Ruys (2010), pp. 158 ff.

[226] ILC (1951), pp. 67–68.

[227] Ibid., p. 39, para. 59.

[228] Ruys (2010), p. 159: force used to '(1) diminish the territory or alter the boundaries of another State; (2) alter internationally agreed lines of demarcation…'.

[229] Ibid.: force used to '(3) disrupt or interfere with the conduct of the affairs of another State; (4) secure changes in the government of another State; or (5) inflict harm or obtain concessions of any sort…'.

[230] Ibid.

was regarded as an objective criterion to draw the distinction between impermissible uses of force and instances of permissible self-defense, one that would rule out a case of 'preventive' self-defense.[231]

Both positions had problems. The first placed too heavy a burden on the victim State to prove the intentions behind the armed attack against it, while the second was based on the erroneous belief that in complex situations it would be easy to identify who attacked first.[232] In this context, the theory of mistake of fact reared its head. Canada argued that the United Nations Security Council's role in making a determination in a given case should include examining the intentions behind the attack, since 'the act or acts which could give cause for a charge of aggression might have been carried out by mistake or by accident', suggesting that such cases should not lead to a determination of aggression or an act of self-defense in response.[233] France pointed out that the principle of priority could give rise to disastrous consequences when force is used 'in special circumstances or in the case of error' and suggested that the phrase 'in the circumstances of each particular case' should be used to overcome this difficulty.[234] Japan agreed that unlawful intent should be part of the analysis of whether a use of force constituted 'aggression':

> That requirement would be justified from the practical as well as from the theoretical point of view. *The possibility could be envisaged of certain illegal acts being committed accidentally without any intention of aggression*; it went without saying that such a case should not be included in the category of aggression.[235]

For its part, Italy argued that some cases might give rise to difficulty in applying the principle of priority, pointing out that the Security Council's role should be exactly to determine the existence of an act of aggression when the first use of force was not committed with *animus aggressionis*:

> Turning to the question of intent, [the Italian delegate] pointed out that the use of certain modern armaments entailed serious dangers for States. What would happen if an accident occurred? As the Syrian representative had stated, bombs might fall accidentally on the territory of a State and cause enormous damage. In such a case, would the State responsible for such bombing be considered as the aggressor through having been the first to use force, or would it be the State which took advantage of those circumstances to launch an attack?[236]

Interestingly, the Italian delegate's statement about 'the State which took advantage of [the accidental bombing] to launch an attack' can be interpreted as referring to a State that resorts to self-defense in response to the described accident. This suggests that such an incident should not, in the Italian position, trigger the right to self-defense.

To resolve the controversy between the principles of intent and priority, the definition of aggression incorporated elements of both into the final text. The annex

---

[231] Ibid.; see Sect. 4.6.3.

[232] Ruys (2010), p. 159.

[233] UN Doc A/AC.134/SR.52-66, p. 27.

[234] Ibid., p. 36.

[235] Ibid., p. 41 (emphasis added).

[236] Ibid., p. 133.

to General Assembly resolution 3314 (XXIX), which contains the Definition of Aggression, now reads as follows in Article 2:

> The first use of armed force by a State in contravention of the Charter shall constitute *prima facie* evidence of an act of aggression although the Security Council may, in conformity with the Charter, conclude that a determination that an act of aggression has been committed would not be justified in the light of other relevant circumstances, including the fact that the acts concerned or their consequences are not of sufficient gravity.[237]

This definition calls for some comments. Under this provision, the first use of force is presumed to constitute aggression unless other circumstances pointed to the opposite conclusion. The Definition establishes that such contrary indications include lack of sufficient gravity. This is consistent with the definition of a *crime* of aggression under Article 8 *bis* of the Rome Statute of the International Criminal Court. Moreover, as pointed out by Ruys after surveying the history of negotiation of this resolution, a lack of hostile intent or *animus aggressionis* may, when taken together with the other circumstances of the case, negate a charge of aggression.[238] Following the logic of a number of statements by States during this process, an instance of genuine and reasonable mistake of fact could fall within this factual paradigm. The statement by the French delegate, in particular, gives the indication that the open phrasing 'in light of other relevant circumstances' is intended to cover this.

At the very least, and without delving too deeply into the question of aggression itself, the author points out that this negotiation suggests that a mistake of fact could, in the proper circumstances, lead to the conclusion that the force used in pursuance of it does not constitute an 'armed attack' for the purposes of Article 51 of the Charter. Perhaps a confirmation of this rule comes from the ICJ's Judgment on the merits of the *Oil Platforms* case. This was a case instituted by Iran against the United States, alleging that the latter's use of force against Iranian oil platforms violated the Treaty of Amity of 1955 between the two States. The United States relied on a series of alleged attacks by Iran against United States-flagged or owned vessels and aircraft to justify a defense of 'necessity' under Article XX (1) (*d*) of the 1955 Treaty of Amity. One of these attacks was allegedly orchestrated by an Iranian vessel, the *Iran Ajr*.[239]

The Court ruled that the use of force by the United States against the Iranian oil installations could only be justified under international law as an act of 'necessity' pursuant to the Treaty of Amity if it complied with the law of self-defense, with which it overlapped in the instant case.[240] The ICJ concluded that no identifiable armed attack had been committed against the United States because the Iranian acts lacked specific *animus aggressionis* directed against the Respondent:

> There is no evidence that the minelaying alleged to have been carried out by the *Iran Ajr*, at a time when Iran was at war with Iraq, was aimed specifically at the United States; and

---

[237] Italics in the original.

[238] Ruys (2010), p. 160.

[239] ICJ (2003), para. 63.

[240] Ibid., para. 43.

> similarly it has not been established that the mine struck by the *Bridgeton* was laid with the specific intention of harming that ship, or other United States vessels. … [T]hese incidents do not seem to the Court to constitute an armed attack on the United States, of the kind that the Court, in the case concerning *Military and Paramilitary Activities in and against Nicaragua*, qualified as a "most grave" form of the use of force…[241]

A similar inference can be drawn from the ICJ's Judgment on the merits in the *Nicaragua* case, where it suggested that the 'possible motivations' of the incursions by Nicaragua into the territories of Honduras and Costa Rica were an essential factor to determine whether they amounted to an 'armed attack' by Nicaragua against either State.[242]

Another possible example of this is an incident that occurred in 1965. An Egyptian plane orchestrated an attack on the Emirate of Beihan, which at the time was part of a British protectorate. When the United Kingdom protested the attack, the authorities of Egypt assured the British Ambassador that its pilots had been ordered not to cross into the Federation of South Arabia; therefore, the attack could have only been the result of a mistake by the pilot. After considering the evidence, the United Kingdom 'concluded that there was a strong presumption that the attacks were due to a pilot's error' and 'decided therefore to accept [Egypt's] explanation of this particular incident.'[243] The author believes that the United Kingdom's decision not to resort to self-defense to this apparent attack might have been grounded in the same rule of international law that has been described in this section. Indeed, lacking a hostile intention, Egypt's mistake did not warrant a forceful response by the United Kingdom.

The conclusions that can be drawn from the aforementioned analysis are as follows. The concept of 'armed attack' as understood under Article 51 and general international law requires the establishment, in the circumstances of the individual case, of a hostile intent to launch an attack against the State that wishes to rely on self-defense (*animus aggressionis*). When this element is lacking (e.g. in accidental or mistaken uses of force), the incident does not rise to the standard of an 'armed attack', described by the ICJ in the *Nicaragua* case as the gravest form of the use of force, triggering the right to self-defense.[244] To this extent, a genuine and reasonable mistake of fact by the allegedly hostile State should be capable of producing this effect, if the evidence as a whole points in this direction.

This limited and carefully circumscribed conclusion, however, needs to be understood in its proper context. The author clarifies again that this section is not addressing the standard to be applied to the prohibition on the use of force itself, as codified under Article 2 (4) of the United Nations Charter. Rather, the author is delving into the distinct concept of an 'armed attack'. The fact that a particular instance of armed force does not qualify as an 'armed attack' does not automatically mean that it is lawful under Article 2 (4) of the Charter or *jus cogens*. The focus here is not on the

---

[241] Ibid., para. 64 (italics in the original).

[242] ICJ (1986), para. 231.

[243] ILC (1978), p. 104, para. 151.

[244] ICJ (1986), para. 191.

legality of the original use of force, but on the permissibility of the responsive force by the victim of the original incident. Thus, the original use of force may well be internationally wrongful and give rise to international responsibility and the duty to make reparation for it, regardless of a mistake of fact, if a justification under the Charter or *jus cogens* is not forthcoming.[245] Moreover, the fact that the incident does not rise to the gravity of an 'armed attack' for the purposes of Article 51 of the United Nations Charter does not mean that the victim State is defenseless: it solely means that this State cannot resort to the use of force in self-defense. A State injured by an incident falling short of an armed attack would be entitled to remedies other than self-defense, such as diplomatic protest and the resort to dispute settlement mechanisms. This distinction is essential for understanding the particular legal effects of a mistake of fact under general international law, and was canvassed in the following terms by the ICJ in *Nicaragua* in the context of collective self-defense:

> In the view of the Court, under international law in force today – whether customary international law or that of the United Nations system – States do not have a right of "collective" armed response to acts which do not constitute an "armed attack".[246]

The application of the theory of mistake of fact in this ambit is grounded on the express language of Article 51 of the Charter, which requires the armed attack to have been directed 'against' the Member invoking self-defense. The Spanish version evokes the same understanding: 'ataque armado *contra* un Miembro'[247] (an armed attack *against* a Member). The French version is even more explicit: it circumscribes the right to self-defense to the case where the responding State was 'l'objet d'une agression armée' (the victim or object of an armed attack). This textual basis suggests that if by a mistake of fact or accident the State in question was not intended as the target of an armed attack, it does not have the right to respond with force, however proportionate the defensive force would have been.

It is important to note that these observations only apply when the mistake of fact negates the *animus aggressionis* against the State seeking to rely on self-defense. Following the statements and precedents cited previously, this will usually be the case when weapons are deployed by accident or when a State falls victim to a one-off attack intended for another State. In contrast, there may be cases that do not fulfil this condition. For instance, the attacker's mistake may be an 'error of motivation'. Imagine a State that intended to use force, but avowedly in self-defense. There, an attack was intended against the victim State, but the *reasons motivating this use of force* were incorrect. Another example could be a case where the mistake leads to protracted or persistent attacks. In these situations, the existence of an intent to attack is revealed by the nature, gravity and scale of the strikes, notwithstanding the mistake. In both paradigms, the author believes that the right to self-defense of the victim State should be preserved because the hostile intent is real, even if the reasons underpinning it may be erroneous. Since there exists a real risk of further

245 See Sect. 4.6.2.

246 ICJ (1986), para. 211.

247 Emphasis added.

prejudice to the territorial integrity or political independence of the victim State, the analysis should focus on whether defensive force is *necessary* to repel or contain the mistaken attack, instead of, or in addition to, resorting to peaceful means like diplomatic protest.[248]

This has sound policy foundations. The purpose of Article 51 of the United Nations Charter is to safeguard the right of States to self-preservation when their territorial integrity or political independence are put at risk by foreign aggression. Granting the same right when the Member is *not* the target of the alleged attack, save for considerations of collective self-defense, would contradict this rationale and find no basis in Article 51 of the Charter. In the words of the ICJ, the incident could not be considered an armed attack *on* the Member in question. This interpretation also serves the purposes of the Charter more generally. It prevents escalation of force when it is not necessary. If *animus aggressionis* is lacking, as described in this section, the incident should be capable of expeditious settlement through diplomatic or other means, without resorting to further armed force. The State victim of a mistaken or accidental attack would retain the right to activate the mechanisms for settlement of disputes to obtain reparation for any damage caused to its territory and its people, since the incident would still constitute a violation of international law.[249] In other words, this interpretation strengthens Article 2 (4)'s prohibition of the use of force and Article 33 (1)'s obligation to resolve disputes peacefully when they are likely to endanger international peace and security.

4.6.5 The Author of the Attack and the Target of Self-defense

The final constellation of cases concerns the use of force in response to an armed attack but against the wrong target. This no longer concerns the existence of the armed attack, its motivation or its gravity, but a situation where the State does have the right to resort to the use of force in individual or collective self-defense. As the ICJ stated in the *Nicaragua,*[250] *Oil Platforms*[251] and *Armed Activities*[252] cases, as well as the *Legality of the Threat or Use of Nuclear Weapons* advisory opinion,[253] the defensive use of force must comply with the elements of necessity and proportionality. In this aspect of the mistake of fact question, there are more numerous judicial pronouncements that could be considered. In the author's view, these cases point to

---

[248] An alternative interpretation would argue that both constellations should be analyzed through the lens of necessity: in the first instance, the forceful response is not necessary and in the second, it is. This reading would have the purpose of preserving the right to self-defense in principle in both cases. Although this alternative interpretation is possible from a theoretical perspective, the author believes that the conceptualization proposed in this book is more in keeping with the State practice.

[249] See Sect. 4.6.2.

[250] ICJ (1986), paras. 176, 194, 237.

[251] ICJ (2003), paras. 51, 68, 73–77.

[252] ICJ (2005), para. 147.

[253] ICJ (1996), para. 41.

the conclusion that an erroneous identification of the target of self-defense defeats the plea due to a lack of necessity.

The key case in this respect is *Oil Platforms*.[254] One of the issues involved in the case was the United States decision to direct its defensive acts against Iranian oil installations instead of a standard military target. When the issue of necessity was addressed as part of self-defense, the United States made the interesting argument that '[a] measure of discretion should be afforded to a party's good faith application of measures to protect its essential security interests.'[255] The ICJ replied in the following terms:

> The Court does not however have to decide whether the United States interpretation of Article XX, paragraph 1 (d) [of the 1955 Treaty of Amity], on this point is correct, since the requirement of international law that measures taken avowedly in self-defence must have been necessary for that purpose is *strict and objective, leaving no room for any "measure of discretion"*.[256]

Having found that the United States had failed to exhaust alternative diplomatic measures before resorting to the use of force and that some of the oil platforms had been regarded as a target of opportunity rather than a 'previously identified … military target', the ICJ concluded that the use of force had not been necessary.[257] In the same vein, in the *Nicaragua* case, the ICJ stated that whether force used allegedly in self-defense was 'necessary' under the 1956 Treaty of Friendship, Commerce and Navigation between Nicaragua and the United States 'was not … purely a question for the subjective judgment of the party'.[258] A further precedent that may support this is the *Dogger Bank* case cited previously,[259] in which the incorrect selection of a target of self-defense attracted international responsibility.

It is clear, then, that the requirement of necessity within the law of self-defense is to be regarded as objective, and 'leaving no room for any "measure of discretion"' to the State that resorts to the use of force. By implication, an error as to the target of the defensive operation negates the element of necessity and frustrates the plea of self-defense.

One aspect of this question that is worth considering is the taking of self-defense measures in the cyber context. There, the Tallinn Manual 2.0 provides in its commentary to rule 71 that self-defense is subject to a 'reasonable determination' about the occurrence of the attack or the identity of the attacker,[260] which is to be assessed based on the contemporaneous evidence, not the information that becomes available later.[261] This language fully endorses the possibility that a mistake of fact might not deprive the State of the possibility of relying on self-defense. Although the policy

---

[254] See Sect. 4.6.4 for the facts of this case.

[255] ICJ (2003), para. 73.

[256] Ibid. (emphasis added).

[257] Ibid., para. 76.

[258] ICJ (1986), para. 282.

[259] See Chap. 3, Sect. 3.2.2.

[260] Emphasis added.

[261] International Group of Experts (2017), Rule 71, para. 23.

behind it is clear, especially considering the difficulty of attributing cyberattacks accurately, the author considers that contrary considerations relating to the strictness with which the use of force should be handled vastly outweigh that policy. Moreover, not only is this position at odds with the views of the ILC and the ICJ but, as was rightly pointed out by Lahmann, it is also not supported by consistent and uniform State practice in the cyber context.[262]

4.7 Consent

The remaining CPW is consent, regulated in Article 20 of the Articles on State Responsibility. This provision reads as follows:

> Valid consent by a State to the commission of a given act by another State precludes the wrongfulness of that act in relation to the former State to the extent that the act remains within the limits of that consent.

In this context, two constellations need to be distinguished.

4.7.1 Putative or Implicit Consent

The first type of case will be termed 'putative consent' and involves a situation in which one State *believes* that another State has granted it consent to pursue a particular course of action that would have otherwise violated an obligation owed to the second State. The answer to this particular constellation lies in what the ILC terms 'implicit consent'.[263] To illustrate this situation, the ILC refers to the 1911 *Savarkar* case, which concerned the arrest and return of Vinayak Savarkar to a British vessel for the purposes of law enforcement. In this case, the British police had alerted to France that Savarkar would be transported to India for the purposes of prosecution on charges of abetting murder, and for that aim he was aboard the vessel *Morea* which would touch at Marseilles a couple of days later. While the vessel was at Marseilles, Savarkar successfully escaped and swam ashore. When this happened, three persons aboard the *Morea* also came ashore to help a French brigadier, who detained Savarkar and returned him to the vessel's crew. A dispute ensued between Britain and France over whether the *Morea* crew who came ashore to assist in Savarkar's arrest had violated French sovereignty.

The arbitral tribunal constituted to rule on the case concluded that no violation had been committed. It pointed out that on receiving the British alert that they would transport Savarkar through Marseilles, the French Ministry of Interior issued instructions to its agents to 'take the measures necessary' to prevent Savarkar from escaping.[264]

[262] Lahmann (2020).

[263] ILC (2001), Art. 24, para. 8.

[264] Arbitral Tribunal (1911), p. 253.

The French brigadier had accepted the help of the *Morea* crew in arresting Savarkar and immediately took the fugitive back to the *Morea*.[265] Thus, 'the persons on board in charge of Savarkar might well have believed that they could count on the assistance of the French Police'.[266] Later, a French Commissaire boarded the vessel and placed himself at the disposal of the *Morea*'s Commander.[267] Moreover, the Prefect of Marseilles sent a telegram a few days letter informing the Interior Minister that he had acted according to the instructions of the Directeur de la Sûreté générale to prevent the escape of Savarkar.[268] Hence, since the brigadier's conduct had not been disclaimed by his chiefs before the *Morea* left Marseilles, 'the British Police might naturally have believed that the brigadier had acted in accordance with his instructions, or that his conduct had been approved'.[269] The tribunal concluded that

> …it is manifest that the case is not one of recourse to fraud or force in order to obtain possession of a person who had taken refuge in foreign territory, and that there was not, in the circumstances of the arrest and delivery of Savarkar to the British Authorities and of his removal to India, anything in the nature of a violation of the sovereignty of France, and that *all those who took part in the matter certainly acted in good faith and had no thought of doing anything unlawful*… [W]hile admitting that an irregularity was committed by the arrest of Savarkar, and by his being handed over to the British Police, *there is no rule of international law imposing, in circumstances such as those which have been set out above, any obligation on the Power which has in his custody a prisoner, to restore him because of a mistake committed by the foreign agent who delivered him up to that Power*.[270]

This case is presented by the ILC as an example in which 'valid consent' was given.[271] This allows us to arrive at some conclusions.

Firstly, in limited circumstances, a mistake of fact by one State as to whether another State has given valid consent may be enough to trigger Article 20 of the ILC Articles. The author believes that this is but a manifestation of the principle of good faith and particularly the rule of acquiescence. This last rule has been described by a Chamber of the ICJ as 'equivalent to tacit recognition manifested by unilateral conduct which the other party may interpret as consent'.[272] It does not require the showing of a detrimental consequence for the State that relies on the putative consent.[273] As the ICJ said in *Temple of Preah Vihear*, this rule attaches when 'the circumstances were such as [to call] for some reaction, within a reasonable period', if the State that created the legitimate expectation 'wished to disagree' with the underlying actions (qui tacet consentire videtur si loqui debuisset ac potuisset).[274]

---

[265] Ibid., p. 254.

[266] Ibid.

[267] Ibid.

[268] Ibid.

[269] Ibid.

[270] Ibid (emphasis added).

[271] ILC (2001), Art. 24, para. 8.

[272] ICJ (1984), paras. 130, 145.

[273] Ibid.

[274] ICJ (1962), p. 23.

Secondly, an inference that another State has given consent should be based on objective and solid grounds. In other words, the mistake of fact needs to be objectively reasonable and based on tangible evidence. The *Savarkar* incident shows that the conduct of France's law enforcement agents demonstrated an attitude from which consent could be inferred, creating a legitimate expectation on the part of Britain.

Thirdly, the fact that the arbitral tribunal examined the grounds on which the British agents made the mistake to arrive at its conclusion shows that the alleged mistake is reviewable. Hence, the action may still be illegal if the consent is found to have been invalid for another reason. Here is where the general rule of objective responsibility comes in. If the State's assessment as to consent turns out to be wrong, it alone is responsible unless the other State acted in such a way as to contribute to the injury[275] or defraud the wrongdoing State, in which case responsibility may be apportioned as appropriate. The possibility of reviewing and even refuting the claim of putative consent is implicit in the ILC's analysis. The ILC repeatedly refers to consent 'given' in respect of the act in question.[276] It also delves into the question of the validity of that consent, including whether the agent that gave it on behalf of the State was authorized to do so.[277] Particularly the reference to '*valid* consent'[278] is intended to guard against cases in which 'consent may not be validly given at all' or is contrary to *jus cogens*.[279] The fact that the conduct needs to fall 'within the limits' of the consent given also points in this direction. Although the rules on the giving of consent in this context differ from those relating to attribution,[280] the similarities between this paradigm and the theories previously explored that may grant some relevance to mistakes of fact, such as the theory of appearance, are worthy of note.[281]

4.7.2 Mistaken Consent

The second category of cases relates to the situation in which the consent given by one State to another was based on a mistake of fact. The author instead terms it 'mistaken consent' for the purposes of distinction. This is a case where the validity of the consent given must be examined. To the extent that the giving of consent involves the State's capacity to make treaties or unilateral declarations,[282] the rule codified in Article 48 of the Vienna Convention on the Law of Treaties may lead to the invalidation (or revocation) of the mistaken consent, if the stringent requirements

[275] See Article 39 of the Articles on State Responsibility.

[276] See e.g. ILC (2001), Art. 24, paras. 1, 2, 3.

[277] Ibid., paras. 4, 5.

[278] Emphasis added.

[279] ILC (2001), Art. 24, para. 7.

[280] Ibid., para. 5.

[281] See Chap. 2, Sect. 2.2.1.

[282] See Chap. 2, Sect. 2.2.2.

found therein are met. Thus, a State that erroneously consents to another State's wrongful act may seek to invalidate or revoke that consent if the mistake of fact 'relates to a fact or situation which was assumed by the State to exist' at the relevant time and 'formed an essential basis of its consent'.

References

Austin JL (1956) A plea for excuses. Proc Aristotelian Soc 57:1–30

Berman M (2003) Justification and excuse, law and morality. Duke Law J 53:1–77

Brunner C (2019) Article 79 [impediment excusing a party from damages]. In: Brunner C, Gottlieb B (eds) Commentary on the UN sales law (CISG). Kluwer Law International, pp 551–559

De Luca MA (2012) Using the air force against civil aircraft. ASPJ Africa & Francophonie

Geiß R (2005) Civil aircraft as weapons of large-scale destruction: countermeasures, article 3BIS of the Chicago convention, and the newly adopted German "Luftsicherheitsgesetz." Michigan J Int L 27:1

Gray C (2008) International law and the use of force, 3rd edn. Oxford University Press

Hentrei S, Soley X (2011) Force majeure. In: Planck M (ed) Encyclopedia of Public International Law. Accessed 26 Aug 2023

International Group of Experts (2017) Tallinn manual 2.0 on the international law applicable to cyber operations, 2nd edn. Prepared by the International Group of Experts at the Invitation of the NATO Cooperative Cyber Defence Centre of Excellence. Cambridge University Press

Ishida Y (2018) CISG article 79: exemption of performance, and adaptation of contract through interpretation of reasonableness? Full of sound and fury, but signifying something. Pace Int Law Rev 30(2):331–382

Klamberg M (2017) Commentary on the law of the international criminal court. Torkel Opsahl Academic EPublisher

Kutoroff A (2016) Excuse in international law. Capital Univ Law Rev 44:189–244

Lahmann H (2020) Mistake of fact in putative self-defence against cyber attacks. https://www.ejiltalk.org/mistake-of-fact-in-putative-self-defence-against-cyber-attacks/. Accessed 16 Aug 2023

Lowe V (1999) Precluding wrongfulness or responsibility: a plea for excuses. Euro J Int Law 10(2):405–411

Milanovic M (2020a) Mistakes of fact when using lethal force in international law: part I. https://www.ejiltalk.org/mistakes-of-fact-when-using-lethal-force-in-international-law-part-i/. Accessed 16 Aug 2023

Milanovic M (2020b) Mistakes of fact when using lethal force in international law: part II. https://www.ejiltalk.org/mistakes-of-fact-when-using-lethal-force-in-international-law-part-ii/. Accessed 16 Aug 2023

Milanovic M (2020c) Mistakes of fact when using lethal force in international law: part III. https://www.ejiltalk.org/mistakes-of-fact-when-using-lethal-force-in-international-law-part-iii/. Accessed 16 Aug 2023

Paddeu F (2012) A genealogy of force majeure in international law. Br Yearbook Int Law 82:381–494

Piéri R (2021) Force Majeure. Jus Mundi. https://jusmundi.com/en/document/wiki/en-force-majeure. Accessed 10 Aug 2021

Randelzhofer A and Dörr O (2012) Article 2 (4). In: Simma B, Khan DE, Nolte G, Paulus A, Wessendorf N (eds) The charter of the United Nations: a commentary. Oxford University Press, pp 200–234

Ruys T (2010) 'Armed attack' and article 51 of the UN charter: evolutions in customary law and practice. Cambridge University Press

Schwenzer I, Hachem P, Kee C (2012) Global sales and contract law. Oxford University Press

Sukumar G (2021) Mistake of fact, interceptive self-defense and right to life. https://silpnujs.wordpress.com/2021/04/27/mistake-of-fact-interceptive-self-defense-and-right-to-life/. Accessed 21 Aug 2023

Szurek S (2010) Chapter 33.5. Circumstances precluding wrongfulness in the ILC articles on state responsibility: force majeure. In: Crawford J, Pellet A, Olleson S, Parlett K (eds) The law of international responsibility. Oxford University Press, pp 475–480

Tladi D (2022) The extraterritorial use of force against non-state actors. Brill

Von der Heydte, FA (1958) Völkerrecht – Ein Lehrbuch. Verlag für Politik und Wirtschaft

Case Law

Arbitral Tribunal (1911) The Savarkar case (Great Britain, France). RIAA XI:243–255

Arbitral Tribunal (1990) Case concerning the difference between New Zealand and France concerning the interpretation or application of two agreements, concluded on 9 July 1986 between the two States and which related to the problems arising from the rainbow warrior affair (30 Apr 1990). RIAA XX:215–284

ICJ (1949a) Reparation for injuries suffered in the service of the United Nations. Advisory Opinion. ICJ Rep 1949:174

ICJ (1949b) Corfu channel case (United Kingdom/Albania). Judgment. ICJ Rep 1949:4

ICJ (1962) Case concerning the temple of Preah Vihear (Cambodia *v.* Thailand). Judgment. ICJ Rep 1962:6

ICJ (1984) Delimitation of the maritime boundary in the Gulf of Maine Area (Canada/United States of America). Judgment. ICJ Rep 1984:246

ICJ (1986) Case concerning military and paramilitary activities in and against Nicaragua (Nicaragua *v.* United States of America). Judgment. ICJ Rep 1986:14

ICJ (1996) Legality of the threat or use of nuclear weapons. Advisory Opinion. ICJ Rep 1996:226

ICJ (1997) Gabčíkovo-Nagymaros project (Hungary/Slovakia). Judgment. ICJ Rep 1997:7

ICJ (2002) Case concerning the land and maritime boundary between Cameroon and Nigeria (Cameroon *v.* Nigeria: Equatorial Guinea intervening). Judgment 2002:303

ICJ (2003) Case concerning oil platforms (Islamic Republic of Iran *v.* United States of America). Judgment. ICJ Rep 2003:161

ICJ (2005) Case concerning armed activities on the territory of the Congo (Democratic Republic of the Congo *v.* Uganda). Judgment. ICJ Rep 2005:168

ICJ (2010) Accordance with international law of the unilateral declaration of independence in respect of Kosovo. Advisory Opinion. ICJ Rep 2010:403

ICJ (2012) Questions relating to the obligation to prosecute or extradite (Belgium *v.* Senegal). Judgment. ICJ Rep 2012:422

ICJ (2022) Allegations of genocide under the convention on the prevention and punishment of the crime of genocide (Ukraine *v.* Russian Federation). Order of 16 Mar 2022 (provisional measures). ICJ Rep 2022:211

ICJ Verbatim Record 2002/2007. Public sitting held on Tuesday 26 February 2002, at 10 a.m., at the Peace Palace, President Guillaume presiding, in the case concerning the land and maritime boundary between Cameroon and Nigeria (Cameroon *v.* Nigeria: Equatorial Guinea intervening)

ICJ Verbatim Record 2002/2020. Public sitting held on Friday 15 March 2002, at 10 a.m., at the Peace Palace, President Guillaume presiding, in the case concerning the land and maritime boundary between Cameroon and Nigeria (Cameroon *v.* Nigeria: Equatorial Guinea intervening)

Nigeria (1999) Counter-memorial of the Federal Republic of Nigeria. In: ICJ, land and maritime boundary between Cameroon and Nigeria (Cameroon *v.* Nigeria: Equatorial Guinea intervening)

Nigeria (2001) Rejoinder of the Federal Republic of Nigeria. In: ICJ, land and maritime boundary between Cameroon and Nigeria (Cameroon *v.* Nigeria: Equatorial Guinea intervening)

International Law Commission (ILC) documents

Ago (1979) Eighth report on state responsibility by Mr. Roberto Ago, special rapporteur—the internationally wrongful act of the state, source of international responsibility. ILC Yearbook 1979, vol II Part 1

Amador G (1956) International responsibility: report by FV García Amador, Special Rapporteur. ILC Yearbook 1956, vol II

Amador G (1958) International responsibility. Third report by FV García Amador, Special Rapporteur. Responsibility of the State for injuries caused in its territory to the person or property of aliens. Part II: the international claim. ILC Yearbook 1958, vol II. UN Doc A/CN.4/111

Crawford (1999) Second report on state responsibility, by Mr. James Crawford, Special Rapporteur. Document A/CN.4/498 and Add 1-4

ILC (1951) ILC Yearbook 1951, vol II

ILC (1973) Report of the international law commission on the work of its twenty-fifth session, 7 May–13 July 1973. ILC Yearbook 1973, vol II. Doc A/9010/Rev.1

ILC (1978) "Force majeure" and "Fortuitous event" as circumstances precluding wrongfulness: survey of state practice, international judicial decisions and doctrine—study prepared by the Secretariat. ILC Yearbook 1978, vol II Part I

ILC (1996) Report of the international law commission on the work of its forty-eighth session, 6 May–26 July 1996, Official Records of the General Assembly, fifty-first session, supplement no. 10. ILC Yearbook, vol II Part Two

ILC (2001) Draft articles on the responsibility of states for internationally wrongful acts, with commentaries thereto. ILC Yearbook 2001, vol II Part Two

ILC (2018) Draft conclusions on subsequent agreements and subsequent practice in relation to the interpretation of treaties, with commentaries. ILC Yearbook 2018, vol II Part Two

ILC (2022) Draft conclusions on identification and legal consequences of peremptory norms of general international law (jus cogens), with commentaries. ILC Yearbook 2022, vol II Part Two

Koskenniemi M (2006) Fragmentation of international law: difficulties arising from the diversification and expansion of international law. UN Doc A/CN.4/L.682

United Nations documents

Documents of the United Nations Conference on International Organization, vol VI Commission I General Provisions. San Francisco 1945 [UNCIO 1945 VI]

Letter dated 5 July 1988 from the Acting Permanent Representative of the Islamic Republic of Iran to the United Nations addressed to the President of the Security Council, UN Doc S/19981

Letter dated 6 July 1988 from the Acting Permanent Representative of the United States of America to the United Nations addressed to the President of the Security Council, UN Doc S/19989

Resolution adopted by the General Assembly on 2 Mar 2022, UN Doc A/RES/ES-11/1

Provisional Verbatim Record of the 2818th Meeting of the Security Council, held at Headquarters, New York on Thursday, 14 July 1988 at 10.30 a.m., UN Doc S/PV.2818

Provisional Verbatim Record of the 2819th Meeting of the Security Council, held at Headquarters, New York on Friday, 15 July 1988 at 10.30 a.m., UN Doc S/PV.2819

Provisional Verbatim Record of the 2820th Meeting of the Security Council, held at Headquarters, New York on Monday, 18 July 1988, at 10.30 a.m., UN Doc S/PV.2820

Summary Records of the 52nd to 33rd Meetings of the 3rd session of the Special Committee on the Question of Defining Aggression (19 Oct 1970) UN Doc A/AC.134/SR.52-66

Legal Instruments

United Nations Convention on Contracts for the International Sale of Goods. 11 Apr 1980. UNTS 1489:3

United Nations Charter. 26 June 1945. UNTS I:1

Miscellaneous

Antigua and Barbuda et al. (2022) Statement 'Continued Support for an End to Russian Aggression in Ukraine' read by the Minister of Foreign Affairs of the Republic of Guatemala, H. E. Mario Adolfo Búcaro Flores, on behalf of and representing the delegations of Antigua and Barbuda, Bahamas, Barbados, Belize, Canada, Chile, Colombia, Costa Rica, Dominican Republic, Ecuador, Grenada, Guatemala, Guyana, Haiti, Jamaica, Panama, Paraguay, Peru, Suriname, Saint Kitts and Nevis, Saint Lucia, Trinidad and Tobago, United States, and Uruguay, during the first plenary session of the fifty-second regular session of the OAS General Assembly, held on October 6, 2022. AG/INF.763/22

Czech Republic (2022) Statement of H. E. Jan Lipavský. Minister of Foreign Affairs of the Czech Republic. https://www.mzv.cz/file/4567551/CZ_MFA_Statement_Minister_Jan_Lipavsky_OSCE_PC_24_February_2022.pdf. Accessed 21 Aug 2023

Deutsche Welle (2023) Fact check: Russia's disinformation campaign targets NATO. https://www.dw.com/en/fact-check-russias-disinformation-campaign-targets-nato/a-64675398. Accessed 21 Aug 2023

European Union (2022) EU Statement regarding Russia's unprovoked and unjustified military aggression against Ukraine. https://www.eeas.europa.eu/eeas/eu-statement-regarding-russia's-unprovoked-and-unjustified-military-aggression-against-ukraine_en. Accessed 21 Aug 2023

Guatemala and Ukraine (2022) Declaración Conjunta del Presidente de Ucrania Volodymyr Zelenskyy y el Presidente de la República de Guatemala Alejandro Eduardo Giammattei Falla. https://www.minex.gob.gt/Noticias/Noticia.aspx?ID=30602. Accessed 21 Aug 2023

Principles on International Commercial Contracts. Institut International pour l'Unification du Droit Privé (UNIDROIT). Version of 2016

United States (2022a) Statement by President Biden on Russia's Unprovoked and Unjustified Attack on Ukraine. https://www.whitehouse.gov/briefing-room/statements-releases/2022/02/23/statement-by-president-biden-on-russias-unprovoked-and-unjustified-attack-on-ukraine/. Accessed 21 Aug 2023

United Nations (2022b) Secretary-general, in statement on Ukraine, Calls Russian Federation's Military Offensive 'wrong, against charter, unacceptable, but not irreversible'. https://press.un.org/en/2022/sgsm21158.doc.htm. Accessed 21 Aug 2023

Chapter 5
Conclusions

5.1 Introduction: Observations to Be Drawn from State Practice and Decisions

Up to this point, the following findings have been made:

(a) In general, the law of State responsibility continues to be solidly grounded on objectivity. The mental state of the State or its agent is not relevant for determining whether a violation of international law has been committed. As a result, in many areas of international law, the doctrine of mistake of fact would appear to be ruled out. However, this general rule is populated by several exceptions.

(b) The first main exception concerns the issue of attribution, the first step in determining whether State responsibility has been triggered. In this context, we see two distinct paradigms. In the first instance, in the field of acts by State agents or non-State actors empowered to exercise elements of governmental authority, a semblance of an official act is enough to trigger the State's responsibility, even if the act was in truth not authorized or exceeded instructions (*ultra vires*). This rule is so broad, that even instances of mistaken identification of official acts may come within its ambit. In the second instance, a mistake of fact may invalidate the acknowledgement and adoption of a conduct under Article 11 of the International Law Commission's (ILC) Articles on State Responsibility, effectively preventing attribution, if the error relates to an essential fact.

(c) The second main exception concerns the second element of State responsibility: the finding of a breach. Here, a mistake of fact may prevent the establishment of international responsibility if the primary rule at play incorporates a subjective or mental element, and only to the extent that the mistake of fact invalidates that element. This includes the case of international criminal law, where intent is required to establish the commission of an international crime, and where mistake of fact is expressly regulated as an exclusion of responsibility under Article 32 of the Rome Statute of the International Criminal Court. If the primary

J. P. Hernández Páez, *Mistake of Fact in Public International Law*,
SpringerBriefs in Law, https://doi.org/10.1007/978-3-031-59508-0_5

rule does not require such a mental element, the general rule is that the material conduct of the State is what matters, regardless of any intention or mistake of fact. Instances of responsibility by catalysis and obligations dependent on due diligence allow for exoneration based on mistakes of fact if the required due diligence is exhausted.

(d) The third main exception concerns circumstances precluding wrongfulness (CPWs), which defend the State against an otherwise well-founded claim of responsibility. As a start, the doctrine of mistake of fact is *not* an independent CPW recognized under customary international law. Moreover, the general rule continues to be that the responsibility of a State (including the establishment of a CPW) is based on objective fact, such that if the State bases a conduct on a unilateral assessment of the situation and that assessment turns out to be incorrect, then the State is responsible and must bear the consequences. However, a limited form of the doctrine of mistake of fact is present in three of the CPWs (consent, force majeure and distress) to differing degrees of efficacy, as described in Chap. 4.

From the State practice examined and the cases cited, the author observes that all cases where mistakes of fact are validated by the system and allowed to display legal effects share a common characteristic. They all appear to be directly or indirectly associated with a manifestation or corollary of the principle of good faith:

(a) **Consent and *pacta sunt servanda*.**

   (i) The logic behind this corollary of good faith is that a State is bound to a treaty obligation that it consented to perform. If that consent is vitiated by a mistake of fact, then the link of obligation is broken, and the State cannot be expected to comply. Thus, we find in Article 48 of the Vienna Convention on the Law of Treaties the rule of error in the realm of treaty law, which proves this assessment. As was explained in Chap. 2, this same logic should extend to acknowledgements and adoptions under Article 11 of the Articles on State Responsibility, with some adjustments. The same rule applies to cases of mistaken consent, as described in Chap. 4.

   (ii) A State is responsible if it fails to perform a treaty due to an error of fact, unless the treaty itself provides (directly or indirectly) that the error should be considered an excuse. Thus, if the treaty assigns legal consequences to a conduct performed with a particular mental state or element, the mistake of fact prevents those legal consequences from coming into effect if it invalidates that mental state or element. For instance, if the Genocide Convention assigns responsibility for genocide if committed with general intent and *dolus specialis*, these legal consequences are invalidated if the alleged crime is committed due to a mistake of fact that negates those manifestations of intent. Article 32 of the Rome Statute of the International Criminal Court confirms this understanding. In obligations involving due diligence, the mistake of fact may be an important factor to determine if this duty of care has been met.

(b) ***Impossibilia nulla obligatio est***. A State cannot in good faith be expected to perform a legal obligation that has become impossible without its fault (*impossibilia nulla obligatio est*). The same rule extends naturally to the case where the impossibility results not from a material impediment, but from the excusable ignorance or misapprehension of a fact that was a necessary precondition for performing the obligation. Thus, as explained in Chap. 4, a mistake of fact could be considered a manifestation of the CPW of force majeure in exceptional cases. In a related sense, a State agent cannot be forced to perform an obligation that would endanger her life. A perception of life-threatening circumstances can be validated by the system if, in the moment, it was impossible to dispel the perception and the harm to be caused by the failure to perform is less detrimental than the reasonably perceived harm that would be avoided. When the harm caused by non-performance does not outweigh the danger to be averted, this perception may be given some legal effect even if it turns out to have been inaccurate.

(c) **Attribution of the conduct of State organs**. The rule that guarantees attribution to a State of *ultra vires* acts committed by its organs is directly connected with the principle of good faith. Indeed, a State cannot invoke its internal law to justify the non-performance of a treaty or the exclusion of State responsibility, in the terms explained throughout this book. Since internal law cannot be invoked, the responsible State cannot claim that there was a mistake of fact committed by its organs or by the victim State regarding the scope of competence or the powers conferred by internal law. International law creates a blanket presumption in favor of attribution here, which would validate and give effect to the perception of attribution, even if that perception turns out to be incorrect.

(d) **Acquiescence**. As explained in a previous chapter, the rule of acquiescence can lead to recognizing forms of putative consent, when there exists a legitimate expectation that consent has been given. Acquiescence, indeed, entails a tacit recognition that is manifested through unilateral conduct, which the other party may interpret as consent. It is linked to the protection of legitimate expectations. This can lead to giving effect to an honest and reasonable perception of consent, even if that perception turns out to be wrong.

The exception that confirms this rule is that, in the context of self-defense, the ICJ has rejected the permissibility of a margin of appreciation to the defending State based on good faith.[1] Thus, mistakes of fact do not further the cause of self-defense, as explained previously in this book.

---

[1] See chapter 4.

5.2 The Theory of Mistake of Fact is a Manifestation of Good Faith

5.2.1 Good Faith and Mistake in Comparative Law

Already in many domestic legal systems, a *subjective* conception of good faith (from *bona fides*, 'honest belief') is capable of validating honest but incorrect beliefs.[2] The principle of good faith can have this effect for beliefs regarding the lawfulness of a particular act or omission, especially to protect legitimate expectations from the retrospective application of the law.[3] Many systems and instruments also guarantee the protection of 'third parties acting in good faith', in situations where that party legitimately believes in an apparent situation.[4] Such will be the case of apparent authority, as laid down in Article 3:201 of the Principles of European Contract Law or Article 2.2.5 (2) of the UNIDROIT Principles on International Commercial Contracts, which loosely correspond to the concept of attribution for *ultra vires* acts in the law of State responsibility. In some domestic laws, the protection of 'third parties acting in good faith' may also protect a buyer that acts in good faith, unaware that the seller does not have ownership over the goods.[5] Indeed, good faith enables a tribunal to draw upon considerations of fairness to temper the strict law, which allows, in certain cases, for reasonable belief or mistake of fact to act as defenses or mitigate responsibility.[6]

5.2.2 Good Faith in the International System

In international law, good faith is a fundamental principle that permeates the performance of all obligations. It is the conceptual basis for the principle of *pacta sunt servanda*,[7] and it is also the foundation of the binding character of unilateral undertakings according to the International Court of Justice (ICJ).[8] The ICJ has given the principle of good faith a special character, as a rule that shapes and informs the performance of existing rules of international law but does not in itself create new obligations.[9] Thus, for instance, Article 26 of the Vienna Convention on the Law of Treaties says that treaties must be performed in good faith. This means that all efforts by a State to perform an international treaty include a prior step of 'good faith

[2] Poillot (2006), paras. 627 et seqq.

[3] Fauvarque-Cosson and Mazeaud (2008), pp. 178, 179.

[4] Ibid., p. 179.

[5] E.g., Sepinuck (2018).

[6] O'Connor (1992), p. 40.

[7] Schmalenbach (2018), para. 15.

[8] ICJ (1974), para. 49.

[9] ICJ (1988), para. 94.

interpretation', as Schmalenbach calls it,[10] where the obligated party must interpret the instrument and ascertain in good faith what conduct is demanded of it under the treaty in question. As was explained previously, other corollaries emerge from good faith as an international law principle that guides political intercourse between States, such as the protection of legitimate expectations through rules like estoppel and acquiescence.

5.2.3 Mistake of Fact as Good Faith

Seen through the lens of good faith, the role played by mistakes of fact becomes clearer. All examples of States that have been able to rely on a mistake of fact have had in common that **the State could be regarded as acting in accordance with good faith**, in areas where that factor is pertinent. The author believes that this is a rule that can be extrapolated, if ever in a limited fashion:

(a) **Observance of international obligations**. Throughout this book, it has been repeated that under the law of responsibility, the performance of international obligations is judged objectively. When the obligation emanates from a treaty, the key factor is the text of the instrument. But in the realm of international law, even the clearest and best-defined treaty text must be interpreted to be performed.[11] And under Articles 26 and 31 of the Vienna Convention, this interpretative operation needs itself to be conducted in good faith.[12] Thus, while international law measures the performance of the obligation in accordance with the material conduct (act or omission) of the State, the measuring instrument would always be the obligation itself as it may have been laid down. In practice, this means that the performance of the obligation always depends, to some extent, on the exercise of good faith by the obligated State that determines the proper way to fulfil the duty that is incumbent on it. Already the ICJ has recognized that a State may have some discretion as to the way it performs an international obligation.[13] The existence of margins of appreciation for the approximate application of treaties was also proposed in the *Gabčíkovo-Nagymaros Project* case.[14] The author believes that this gives the obligated State a degree of discretion that may, in appropriate cases, open the door for a limited form of the mistake of fact doctrine, without importing overtly subjective elements and thereby maintaining coherence with the secondary norms of responsibility.
(b) **International norms establishing overriding presumptions**. Presumptions based on good faith are fertile ground for the application of the mistake of fact

[10] Schmalenbach (2018), para. 46.
[11] Dörr (2018), para. 14.
[12] Schmalenbach (2018), para. 46.
[13] ICJ (1951), p. 82.
[14] ICJ (1997), para. 67.

doctrine. From the notion that State organs always render their States accountable or that third States can rely on tacit consent, these rules that branch off the principle of good faith tend to create blanket legal presumptions that allow for inferences of fact to be validated even when they may be ruled incorrect later. What has been observed for acquiescence and issues of attribution, could easily be extended to other manifestations of good faith, like the principle of estoppel (*venire contra factum proprium*).

(c) **Higher values associated with good faith**. Some rules that are distilled from the principle of good faith defend what can be described as 'higher values' within the international system. The key examples explored in this book include the principle that impossible obligations are not binding, or the notion that State agents are entitled to avert the performance of life-threatening obligations. These are indissolubly linked to specific CPWs, as discussed in Chap. 4 (force majeure and distress, respectively). The author believes that in such cases the principle of good faith requires that these higher values be protected, even if the material facts that give rise to their application are not fully forthcoming. This could perhaps be described as an analogical or *mutatis mutandis* application of the same values, where they are functionally fulfilled. Some instances of mistake of fact can be subsumed within this paradigm. An obligation that has become impossible to perform due to excusable ignorance or misapprehension of facts is no less impossible than one that has been met with a material impediment. A circumstance that reasonably appears life-threatening and which gives no time for deliberation or discernment is no less threatening than an actual danger to life. The law cannot adopt a formalistic approach to the demonstration of these grounds when doing so would endanger the 'higher values' that the underlying secondary norms were meant to embody.

5.3 Overall Conclusions

What has been described in this final chapter is intended by the author to be a distillation of the State practice and decisions evaluated throughout. They are an interpretation of how the doctrine of mistake of fact may be operationalized without endangering the certainty of the international system as we understand it. The overarching tendencies described in this chapter are intended as an initial proposal as to the significance of mistakes of fact in our discipline and as an invitation for further scrutiny into this emerging aspect of international responsibility. What is revealed by the considerations throughout this book is that the codification of the law of State responsibility, while helpful and generally reflective of current consensus, is by no means complete. Substantive work needs to be done to account for lacunae that may appear theoretically irrelevant or even conquered, but which give rise to uncertainties that make all the difference in the relations between sovereign States and international organizations. The doctrine of mistake of fact is but an example of these emerging elements.

References

Dörr O (2018) Article 31. General rule of interpretation, 2nd edn. In: Dörr O, Schmalenbach K (eds) Vienna convention on the law of treaties: a commentary. Springer, pp 559–616

Fauvarque-Cosson B, Mazeaud D (2008) European contract law: materials for a common frame of reference: terminology, guiding principles, model rules. Sellier

O'Connor JF (1992) Good faith in international law. Dartmouth

Poillot E (2006) Droit européen de la consummation et uniformisation du droit des contrats. LGDJ 463

Schmalenbach K (2018) Article 26. Pacta Sunt Servanda, 2nd edn. In: Dörr O, Schmalenbach K (eds) Vienna convention on the law of treaties: a commentary. Springer, pp 467–492

Sepinuck SL (2018) The various standards for the 'good faith' of a purchaser. Bus Lawyer 73(3):581–626

Jurisprudence

ICJ (1951) Haya de la Torre case (Colombia/Peru). Judgment. ICJ Rep 1951:71

ICJ (1974) Nuclear tests case (New Zealand *v*. France). Judgment. ICJ Rep 1974:457

ICJ (1988) Border and transborder armed actions (Nicaragua *v.* Honduras). Jurisdiction and Admissibility. ICJ Rep 1988:69

ICJ (1997) Gabčíkovo-Nagymaros project (Hungary/Slovakia). Judgment. ICJ Rep 1997:7

Index

J. P. Hernández Páez, *Mistake of Fact in Public International Law*,
SpringerBriefs in Law, https://doi.org/10.1007/978-3-031-59508-0

The manufacturer's authorised representative in the EU is Springer Nature Customer Service Centre GmbH, Europaplatz 3, 69115 Heidelberg, Germany. If you have any concerns regarding our products, please contact ProductSafety@springernature.com

Printed and bound by CPI Group (UK) Ltd, Croydon, CR0 4YY
23/09/2026
02221543-0011